DANTE

Monarchy

TRANSLATED AND EDITED BY
PRUE SHAW

Senior Lecturer in the Italian Department
University College London

CAMBRIDGE
UNIVERSITY PRESS

CAMBRIDGE
UNIVERSITY PRESS

University Printing House, Cambridge CB2 8BS, United Kingdom

Published in the United States of America by Cambridge University Press, New York

Cambridge University Press is part of the University of Cambridge.

It furthers the University's mission by disseminating knowledge in the pursuit of
education, learning and research at the highest international levels of excellence.

www.cambridge.org
Information on this title: www.cambridge.org/9780521567817

First published 1996
Twelfth printing 2010

A catalogue record for this publication is available from the British Library

ISBN 978-0-521-56781-7 Paperback

To the memory of my father

ROBERT ALLAN SHAW

who founded the first Italian Department in an Australian University
and who taught me to love Dante

Contents

Acknowledgement

This book reproduces the English translation, and an abridged version of the introduction and notes, of Dante, *Monarchia*, the fourth volume in the series Cambridge Medieval Classics, where the English version is printed facing the Latin text, and is accompanied by a Latin index, a Map of the World according to Orosius, and a more extensive bibliography.

Introduction

Why read the *Monarchy*, Dante's treatise on political theory? A minor work by one of the world's great poets, written in the moribund language which he wisely rejected in favour of the vernacular when writing at full creative pressure, argued in a manner which can seem needlessly pedantic and repetitive in its procedures and its formulations, it expresses ideas which have been described as backward-looking, utopian and even fanatical. Yet a recent book on the political thought of the period can unselfconsciously refer to the *Monarchy* as a masterpiece,[1] and it is surely a text of remarkable interest. The originality and power of the political vision it embodies, the passion with which that vision is experienced and expressed, shine through the alien language and the alienating methodology. The small effort the text requires of its modern readers is amply repaid by the sense it conveys of a man passionately engaged in the political debates of his age, but equally passionate in his determination that the pressure of present concerns should not blind us to underlying principles. Only a grasp of universal truths about human beings and human life will furnish an answer to the fundamental question of how people should live together and what form of political organization best suits human nature.

The attempt to argue from first principles is one of the most strikingly original aspects of the *Monarchy*, but it is not a work of ivory-tower idealism, of theory divorced from political experience. Dante had been actively involved in the political life of Florence in

[1] Antony Black, *Political Thought in Europe 1250–1450*, Cambridge 1992, p. 96.

the closing years of the thirteenth century and the early years of the fourteenth; he had enrolled in a Guild in order to be eligible for public office, had served on important councils, and had been elected in due course as one of the six priors who governed the city for periods of two months at a time. In October 1301 he had been sent as one of three ambassadors representing the commune to the papal curia in Rome, on a peace-keeping mission to Pope Boniface VIII, whose aggressive and duplicitous intervention in the affairs of Dante's native city threatened its independence and stability. He was never to see Florence again. As the competing factions within the Guelf party which controlled the city manoeuvred for power, a trumped-up charge of corruption in office was brought against him in his absence; the Black Guelfs had secretly made a treacherous alliance with the unscrupulous pope and so were able to oust the Whites (of whom Dante at this stage was one). A decree of January 1302 condemned him to a large fine, two years banishment from Tuscany and permanent exclusion from public office. The fine remaining unpaid within the stipulated three days, in March he was condemned to death at the stake should he ever return.

A political exile for the remaining twenty years of his life, he travelled throughout Italy, observing at first hand the devastating effects of factional intrigue and papal meddling in temporal affairs. What he had already experienced directly in Florence – public disorder, lawlessness, treachery, lust for power subverting any possibility of peaceful and orderly public life conducted according to principle and not shameless self-interest – he now saw as endemic to the whole country. His horizons broadened in exile to the point where he no longer identified himself with any political grouping, although the pro-imperial stance of his later years is closer to the Ghibellines than the Guelfs. Whether he wrote the *Monarchy* while there was still hope that the Holy Roman Emperor Henry VII could unite Italy (and provide effective secular leadership for a country whose fragmentation into smaller political units and endless internecine warfare were exploited by a ruthlessly ambitious papacy), or whether he wrote it after these hopes had evaporated, is a question to which scholarship can give only a conjectural answer. But it is certain that when Dante engages with the centuries-long debate on the relative powers of pope and emperor (or 'monarch', as Dante usually calls him), his conclusions are born of direct and bitter experience.

In this sense, then, the *Monarchy* is not a work of theory divorced from practical experience of politics; rather, it grows out of painful personal experience of political life, and a thwarted desire to participate effectively in the public life of his native city. In another sense, though, the treatise is purely theoretical. Dante is arguing about principles and the conclusions to be drawn from them. The arguments are abstract, concerned to elucidate fundamental truths. At no point does he consider how his conclusions might be implemented in practice. Where Aristotle famously collected and examined the constitutions of 158 city-states as a preliminary to the elaboration of his *Politics*, and frequently refers to specific instances of actual political practice, Dante's argument is conducted on a different plane altogether, and can seem curiously devoid of concrete detail. He is interested not in how things are, but how they ought to be, though how they ought to be reflects, at a more profound level, how they really are, being based on a true understanding of human nature.

Although he is treading well-trodden ground – the relationship of papacy and empire is the central subject of political debate in the later Middle Ages – Dante's conclusions are entirely his own. This is especially true of the first two books of the treatise. Each of the three books addresses one of the issues identified in the opening pages as a source of confusion and therefore a proper subject of investigation: Is monarchy necessary to the well-being of the world? Did the Roman people take on the office of the monarch by right? Does the monarch derive his authority directly from God, or from some other source? Book I offers us a meditation on political theory, Book II an interpretation of human history, and Book III a contribution to the most fiercely debated political issue of Dante's own lifetime, the role of the papacy in relation to secular power.

The arguments developed in the first book to prove that mankind is best governed by a single world-ruler or monarch, whose sovereignty and jurisdiction encompass and override those of all lesser kingdoms and their rulers, are largely derived from Aristotle. But before these arguments can be advanced and defended, a principle must be established which provides the point of reference to which we return for validation and confirmation that our arguments are sound. (Each of the books will start with the enunciation of such a principle: the sense of an ordering and shaping intelligence which imposes a meaningful pattern on complex material is strong throughout. There is no point, Dante will remind us later, again echoing Aristotle, in arguing with those who deny first principles.)

The principle enunciated in the first book is this: mankind considered as a totality has its own function or purpose, a purpose which cannot be fulfilled by any individual, however brilliant, or by any single group or race, however gifted, but only by the whole of humanity considered precisely as a whole. That purpose is to realize human intellectual potential, *simul* (all at once) and *semper* (all the time). Man is set above the animals by his capacity to reason, and below the angels by the limitations placed on that capacity by his earthly body. His knowledge of the world comes to him through his senses; his reason interprets the data they supply. It is man's unique hybrid status in the created world – the combination in him, and in him alone, of mind and body – which defines his essential nature and identifies humanity's purpose, whose fulfilment is thus a collective enterprise. The means necessary to achieve this goal is peace, for only peace enables human beings to realize their potential fully and continuously.

Any collective enterprise will require an individual to lead, guide and direct those engaged in it. This is true of any social grouping, from the smallest (the individual household or extended family) to the largest (the *regnum*). Here Dante is closely following Aristotle, whose authority he explicitly invokes, but for Aristotle the city-state was the largest political entity. Dante adds the kingdom to Aristotle's list, following medieval theorists like Aquinas and Giles of Rome, and reflecting the political reality of medieval Europe, where the independent Italian communes or city-republics provided a parallel to the Greek city-state, but where larger kingdoms included many cities within their borders. Dante's final step brings him to a conclusion which is not Aristotelian at all: if humanity as a whole is engaged in a collective enterprise, it too will need a leader or ruler to ensure that it achieves its goal. A single sovereign authority set over all lesser rulers is thus a logical necessity, given the nature of human beings and the purpose of their lives.

A first group of arguments in support of this thesis turns on the ordering or structuring of reality, and the relationship of that ordering to final ends or goals. Again the argument is Aristotelian, but the conclusion is not. Wholes consist of the sum of their parts and are prior to and superior to any single constituent element.

This is true of any aspect of the natural world (of the human body, for example; of an army; of any political grouping of whatever size). If we consider humanity as a whole made up of lesser parts (kingdoms, cities, communities, families), we find that each of these parts requires a leader; logically then the whole must also require a leader. Equally and inversely, if we consider humanity as one part of a larger whole (the universe or created world), then again we find that a single ordering principle operates in the cosmos; it ought also therefore to operate in each of its component parts, of which the human race is one. Humanity so ordered will most closely resemble God, by mirroring the principle of oneness or unity of which he is the supreme example. The analogy from macrocosm to microcosm (which lies at the centre of Book I) is now extended to include the concept of law: just as the whole sphere of heaven, which contains the created universe in Ptolemaic astronomy, is governed by a single movement (that of the Primum Mobile) and a single source of motion (God), so the human race is best ordered if it reflects this pattern or structure by having a single ruler and a single law emanating from him.

A second group of arguments addresses the issues raised by this first intimation of the monarch's function, which is that of peacekeeper and lawgiver. Without a world-ruler there will be no way of resolving the conflicts which inevitably arise among lesser kings and princes competing for territory and power. There must be a supreme authority capable of resolving such disputes or else mankind is condemned to endemic conflict. The resolution of conflict must be just, but the person most able to enact justice is a worldruler: his will alone will not be incapacitated by greed or acquisitiveness, and his power, being absolute, can ensure that justice is enforced. The meticulous examination of the concepts of justice, volition, appetition, power, greed, love, and their complex interrelationships, is grounded in Aristotle; the conclusion is Dante's own.

The function of the monarch is next clarified in relation to freedom. Freedom, which comes from free will, is the source of human happiness both on earth and in the afterlife. The human race is at its best when it is most free. But it is most free when it is governed by a world-ruler, because only then does humanity exist for its own sake. This fundamental point about autonomy and means and ends takes us to the heart of Dante's argument: laws and legislators, political regimes and those who wield power in them, exist for the sake of the citizens and not vice versa. Their power should be neither a means to personal aggrandizement, nor an end in itself, but a means to ensure that their fellow human beings can achieve self-fulfilment individually and collectively. Only a world-ruler can guarantee this. Dante draws on Aristotle in identifying three forms of faulty or perverted government (tyranny, oligarchy and mob-rule), under which men do not exist for their own sake, but become instruments serving some other end (the interests of the tyrant, the few in power, or the mob). Under the overlordship of a world-ruler these three forms of government (the rule of one, of a few, of the majority) can function as they ought and aim at freedom, and thus the happiness and self-fulfilment of their subjects. The monarch as overlord will be best able to dispose other kings and princes, for he alone can, by virtue of his role, be free of greed, which perverts judgment and obstructs justice.

The monarch's function as lawgiver is next considered in terms of the Aristotelian principle of efficiency or economy of effort. The unnecessary multiplication of means is bad: what can be achieved by a single agent is better so achieved. The law must come from a single source, even though in practice there will be regional variations in the implementation of laws to accord with local circumstances.

Dante's final argument is the argument from unity. We come full circle back to our first principle, humanity's collective endeavour, but now seen in terms of how wills can most effectively be directed collectively. Again the reasoning is Aristotelian: unity is logically prior to goodness; humanity as a whole is a kind of concord, and concord is a good; concord therefore has its root in unity; thus the collective will of humanity requires a single guide, and this need can only be met in the person of a world-ruler.

Aristotle's science provides the view of the world which underpins Dante's political theory, which is grounded in Aristotelian notions of causation, potentiality, priority, number, and order. But Dante owes to Aristotle not just his assumptions about the nature of the world and the way it is to be described and understood, but also the methodology of his treatise. The discipline of Aristotelian formal logic underpins Dante's argument in this sense, providing the procedures and the terminology around which it is constructed: the sense of how an investigation should be conducted and what constitutes a sound argument; the need to agree first principles and use syllogistic reasoning to reach conclusions whose validity is unimpugnable; the technique of disposing of opponents' arguments by identifying and naming the fallacies they embody. Paradoxically, if one were asked to nominate the single medieval text which throws most light on the *Monarchy*, it would have to be not the Latin version of the *Politics* (of which Dante may or may not have had first-hand knowledge), nor even William of Moerbeke's translation of the *Ethics* (which he certainly knew, along with Aquinas' commentary on it), but the *Summule logicales* of Petrus Hispanus (later Pope John XXI), a work which not only details with painstaking thoroughness the procedures of dialectic and disputation, but also functions as a compendium of definitions of the basic concepts of Aristotelian philosophy (genus, species, substance, accident, agent, patient, generation, corruption, form, matter, the four kinds of cause and the five kinds of priority).

Dante of course sees Aristotle through a Christian filter – the filter of his own Catholic faith, his knowledge of the Bible and the writings of the church fathers, the commentaries on Aristotle of Aquinas and others. Although there are striking points of convergence between Aristotelian and Christian thinking on such central questions of ethics as *cupiditas* and its destructive role in human social life, there is little in the arguments of Book I that is specifically Christian – even the argument from the unity of God and the discussion of free will have Aristotelian parallels. But if we look at the opening and closing chapters which frame these central arguments the Christian focus is insistent and determining.

The opening chapter, in which Dante explains his purpose, is rich in biblical allusions, explicit and implicit. The fruit-bearing tree, the buried talent, the disinterested pursuit of truth with no thought of financial gain, the prize honourably won and bringing deserved glory, the confident trust in help from on high: all these are resonant images for a reader familiar with the Bible. Indeed the opening words of the treatise reveal the quintessential amalgam of Aristotelianism and Christianity which is to be its most distinctive feature. The Aristotelian observation that all men have a natural desire to know – already used by Dante as the opening sentence of another work, the *Convivio* : 'As the Philosopher says at the beginning of the *Metaphysics*, all men naturally desire to have knowledge' – is here expressed in terms of their relationship to their maker, for it is God who has 'stamped' or 'imprinted' human beings with this love of knowledge.

The final chapter of Book I, where the philosophical arguments are for the first time linked to history, is marked by the same fervent sense of Christian witness. We are reminded of that moment in time when humanity did briefly enjoy universal peace, when the world was ruled as God intended it should be and a universal monarchy existed: the moment of Christ's birth under the reign of Augustus. The chapter ends with an impassioned apostrophe to the human race to recognize the error of its ways and heed the lessons of philosophy, of history and of Scripture (which correspond in broad terms, as we shall see, to the three books of Dante's treatise). With perfect symmetry Book I closes, as it had opened, with a quotation from the Psalms.

Book II is a powerful, poetic, if at times perplexing, demonstration or 'proof' of Dante's deeply held conviction that the role of the Roman empire in human history was crucial, its successful world domination a part of God's providential plan for mankind, and its authority therefore legitimate and legitimately exercised. The monarchy described in Book I is no idealized philosophical abstraction, but a concrete reality which once existed and could exist again. Dante now draws extensively on the work of historians, especially Orosius and Livy (although his knowledge of Livy may not be firsthand). But also, and arrestingly, he draws on the classical poets Virgil and Lucan, whose great epic poems the *Aeneid* and the *Pharsalia* are repeatedly cited as uniquely valuable testimony for the role in human history of the city and people whose story they celebrate. While the historians are mentioned briefly and by way of corroboration, the poets are quoted verbatim and their words are made central. These poetic fragments set into the prose text give an absolutely distinctive character to this book, a resonance and intensity which set it off both from what precedes and what follows. Pagan poetry stands alongside the Bible as true testimony to God's intentions: the *Aeneid* becomes, in Bruno Nardi's memorable phrase, 'la Bibbia dell'Impero', the Bible of the Empire. Where

Book I was dominated by the Philosopher, Book II will be dominated by the Poet.

The structure of Book II is pleasingly symmetrical. At its heart are seven chapters of Roman history – not an orderly account, and only approximately chronological – organized around themes according to the development of Dante's argument. They are flanked by two introductory chapters which lay down principles and procedures, and two concluding chapters which bring us back to the point we had reached at the end of Book I. Book I invited us to contemplate humanity's place in the natural order in the timeless present of philosophical speculation; it anchored those abstractions to history only in the last chapter. Now we approach that same turning-point in time from the opposite direction, as we consider episodes and figures in Roman history from the legendary origins of the city to the reign of Augustus, and seek to understand their significance. Pagan history is presented as an indispensable element in a Christian understanding of the world, only truly intelligible when seen in this perspective. But equally and conversely the full significance of Christ's mission on earth only becomes apparent when seen against the pagan background. We must see Christ's birth and death not simply in terms of redemption and salvation, as theology teaches us to; not simply as the culmination of two thousand years of biblical history, with the New Testament fulfilling the prophecies of the Old; but as events which give the stamp of divine approval to a secular institution, the empire, and which thus have profound implications for our understanding of how the world should be governed – in short, for political theory.

Dante starts, as we have seen him do in Book I, by enunciating a general principle whose truth is self-evident, and on which his whole argument will be based: what God wills in human society is right. To prove that the Roman empire was founded on right we must therefore prove that God willed it. We must not however expect the same degree of certainty in pursuing this line of enquiry (another Aristotelian principle Dante will remind us of more than once as he proceeds). God's will is revealed through his works: in the words of St Paul 'the will of God in itself is indeed invisible; but the invisible things of God "are clearly perceived by being understood through the things he has made" ' [*voluntas quidem Dei per se invisibilis est; et invisibilia Dei 'per ea que facta sunt intellecta conspiciuntur'*]. The wax-and-seal metaphor for the relationship of Creator to creation which has been implicit from the opening sentence of the treatise becomes the central metaphor in Book II, which invites us to contemplate the course of Roman history and see in it clear and unmistakable signs of God's will in operation. Dante now argues not just from principles to conclusions, but from events to their meaning. To determine their meaning we need, in addition to Aristotle's philosophy, the theological notions of the miracle and the *iudicium Dei*.

The first three arguments can be summarized as the argument from nobility (ch. iii); the argument from miracles (ch. iv); and the argument from Roman civic unselfishness (ch. v). The Romans deserved their world dominion because of their nobility, their inherent superiority as a race. The argument is a syllogistic one, which correlates rightful dominion or overlordship with natural distinction. The major premiss ('it is appropriate that the noblest race should rule over all the others') is quickly proved by reference to Aristotle, with supporting testimony from Juvenal and the New Testament. The minor premiss ('the Roman people was the noblest') requires a much more extended survey of the evidence. It is presented as an argument about origins: Aeneas was the father of the Roman people, as both Livy and Virgil agree. His nobility can be measured on three parameters, personal, ancestral and matrimonial. No fewer than nine quotations from the *Aeneid* substantiate these claims.

The argument from miracles gives us direct evidence of God's will. Certain famous episodes in Roman history must be understood as divine interventions in the natural course of events: when the holy shield fell from the sky in the reign of Numa, successor to Romulus, marking the site of the empire that was to arise; when the Capitol under siege by the Gauls was saved by the goose whose cackling awakened the temple guard; when a sudden hailstorm at the critical moment threw the enemy troops into confusion during the siege of Hannibal; when Cloelia escaped from her captors and swam the Tiber to safety during the siege of Porsenna. Dante's interpretation of these episodes as miracles is consciously though not explicitly polemical. Augustine, for example, in the *De civitate Dei* had been scathing about the role of the geese in saving Rome:

'Having extremely sharp ears and extremely fast legs, at the scream of the geese they [i.e. the gods of Ilium] were back in a flash to protect at least the Capitoline Hill, which had escaped capture. Too bad that the warning was heard too late to save the rest of the city!'[2] Where Augustine belittles with irony, Dante uses Virgil's lines on the saving of the Capitol to engage us imaginatively and emotionally with a sense of the miraculous.

The argument from Roman selflessness turns on the relationship between right and the good of the community. The conduct of Roman institutions and citizens in pursuit of the common good is a pursuit of right. The great Romans lived by the ideals expressed in Book I: the suppression of greed, the pursuit of peace and liberty. The litany of famous names of Roman heroes who sacrificed personal advancement and even their lives to the good of the community – Cincinnatus, Fabritius, Camillus, Brutus, Mutius, the Decii – makes stirring reading, culminating in the memory of Cato, whose suicide is for Dante (paradoxically, for suicide is a sin) a supreme example of heroic self-sacrifice in the name of liberty. (Again it is illuminating to compare this with Augustine's less than enthusiastic account in the *De civitate Dei* : 'Of Cato's action I must say, in the first place, that his own friends, some of them learned, very wisely tried to dissuade him from his action, and judged it to be the action of a cowardly rather than a brave spirit.'[3]) The chapter concludes with the demonstration of the technical point that in aiming at right the Romans behaved rightfully, legitimately. Aristotle's logic and philosophy come briefly to centre stage again, though in fact we have never lost sight of either of them, for the syllogistic method remains the chief principle of organization of Dante's rich material, which continues to be informed by Aristotelian notions of causation and purpose.

We have now reached the central chapter of Book II. The argument is from nature's provisions: it is right to preserve what nature has ordained, for nature orders things according to their capacities, and this is the basis of right in the natural world. The principle of Book I – humanity's collective purpose – is fitted into a cosmic framework. Humanity must fulfil its goal if nature is to fulfil her

[2] *De civitate Dei* 3, 8.
[3] *De civitate Dei* 1, 23.

broader purpose, to which it is a necessary means and of which it is a necessary part. Nature's purpose requires a multiplicity of people and nations, and this in turn means there must be a ruling nation. Certain nations are born fitted to rule, others to be subservient (Aristotle confirms this). Nature herself fitted the Romans to rule (and this is confirmed by Virgil). The seal is triumphantly set on the argument with two quotations from the *Aeneid*, including what may well be the most majestic lines in the poem, where Anchises foretells to Aeneas the future glory of the Roman empire: not chance, but destiny; no mere accident of time and circumstance, but Providence in operation. The Philosopher and the Poet come together with compelling force at the heart of Book II, which is the heart of the whole treatise.

The next three chapters take a more problematical approach to the question of how God's will is to be detected. Ch. vii reviews the varied ways in which that will has been revealed to human beings, based on the evidence to be gleaned from biblical accounts. Of the many forms of revelation outlined, two lend themselves to Dante's purposes, both involving strenuous competitive effort. These are the race and the *duellum*: the race between athletes competing in the arena to win a prize, and single combat or trial by champion. We are now invited to recognize both these forms of revelation operating in Roman history.

Chapter viii surveys the history of the ancient world before Roman supremacy was achieved, showing how earlier attempts at global domination – by the Assyrians, the Egyptians, the Persians, Alexander of Macedon – all failed. Only the Romans succeeded; they won the race. The point is underscored with the testimony of poets (Virgil, Lucan and Boethius all testify to the fact of Roman world domination) and of the evangelist St Luke, whose Gospel tells how Augustus decreed that a universal census should be drawn up, reflecting the reality of Roman imperial power.

Chapter ix develops the argument from *duellum* or trial by combat, a concept Dante applies not just to single combat but to any armed engagement which observes certain strict rules. (It must be a solution of last resort; it must be freely agreed on by both parties; and it must be motivated solely by a passionate concern for justice.) From the prehistory of the city, through the early battles with local tribes (the Albans, the Sabines and the Samnites), up to the great wars with foreign enemies (the Greeks and the Carthaginians), the decisive armed encounters in Roman history are seen as a form of trial by combat, their favourable outcome a divine judgment (*iudicium Dei*). The notion of trial by champion as a way of resolving disputes between nations is both biblical and classical: David and Goliath have their counterpart in Aeneas and Turnus, whose single combat to settle the conflict between the Romans (as they will become) and the Rutuli is the climactic encounter at the end of the *Aeneid*.[4] The fight between the Roman and Alban triplets as recounted by Livy is a second key episode in early Roman history which conforms to the pattern of trial by combat, extending the notion to evenly matched teams rather than individuals. (Again we can compare Augustine's account, which emphasizes the barbarity of this episode when judged by Christian or even just by humane standards.[5]) We may baulk at Dante's equating the Second Punic War with single combat – his interpretative grid sits uncomfortably with our sense of history – but for a believer there must presumably be a sense in which the outcome of any battle is a *iudicium Dei*.

Dante has now completed his survey of Roman history. He has evoked the great episodes and the great figures, in an allusive rather than a discursive way, his account built around poetic testimony which conveys with extraordinary power the sense of destiny, mission and greatness of the Roman empire. In the last two chapters of Book II there is a change in direction. He will now argue, he tells us, not from rational principles, as he has largely done hitherto, but from principles of the Christian faith. Two related and parallel

---

[4] Interestingly, in Dante's chronology these two events are almost contemporaneous: see *Convivio* IV, v, 6 ('David was born and Rome was born at the same time') and the commentaries of Busnelli-Vandelli and Vasoli *ad loc.* Single combat or trial by champion has a minor role in the history of medieval warfare, yet it appears to have had a long history as a concept or ideal if not as a reality. William the Conqueror is reported by William of Malmesbury to have offered King Harold the chance of resolving their differences by single combat; Harold refused (cited by G. Neilson, *Trial by Combat*, Glasgow 1890, p. 29); Louis VI of France challenged Henry I of England to single combat; he also refused (cited in P. Contamine, *War in the Middle Ages* (translated by M. Jones), Oxford 1984, p. 41; other examples on pp. 260–1). Almost eight hundred years later Tolstoy surveying the carnage of the Crimean war in Sebastopol wondered whether single combat would not be a less destructive and no more arbitrary way of settling disputes between nations than full-scale war (Leo Tolstoy, *The Sebastopol Sketches*, translated by D. McDuff, London 1986, p. 60).

[5] *De civitate Dei* 3, 14.

arguments echo the close of Book I, both in their content and in their climactic force. Again we are reminded of the point at which Christ entered human history, the moment of contact between divinity and humanity. If Roman imperial authority had not been legitimate, then not only would Christ by his birth have sanctioned an injustice, but the Crucifixion would not have been a true punishment in Christ's person for the sin of Adam, and humanity would not have been redeemed. The coinciding of Christ's birth with the peaceful reign of Augustus is a fact of history whose importance had been emphasized by Augustine's contemporary Orosius in his *Seven Books of History against the Pagans*, but Dante goes far beyond his source in the significance he attaches to it and the conclusions he draws.

There is a sense in which Books I and II are merely a prelude to Book III, a preliminary exercise preparing the ground for Dante's main thesis. In Book III he engages directly with the arguments of papal and imperial polemicists on the central political issue of his age: the relationship of religious to secular power, the relative autonomy of pope and emperor. In the main body of this book he considers and rebuts arguments for the primacy of papal authority and the dependence of the imperial office on the pope: six arguments based on the scriptures; two based on historical actions of emperors and popes; and a final argument from reason. Before engaging with his opponents, he not only establishes his first principle (just as he had done in the first two books), but also carefully identifies exactly who his argument is addressed to. His first chapter is a restatement of his faith in his mission, now emphasizing not its difficulty (as in I, i) but its danger, implicitly evoked by the opening epigraph (which reminds us that Daniel remained unharmed in the lions' den because of his righteousness, his *iustitia*), and reinforced with an extraordinary density of scriptural allusion suggesting combativeness and risk. Dante presents himself as a gladiator armed with shield and breast-plate – the shield of divine power which protects those who defend the truth, the breast-plate of faith – who fights in defence of truth and who must actively cast out the wicked and the lying from the arena.

The first principle on which his arguments are now to be based is this: what is contrary to nature's intention is against God's will. This principle is proved by default (in technical terms, by an argu-

ment *ad impossibile*), i.e. by showing that patently absurd consequences would follow if its opposite were true. Dante's task will be
to show that if the emperor were subject to the pope's authority,
this would be in conflict with nature's intention and hence with
God's will. The special difficulty of this subject is emphasized: the
matter is so fiercely disputed that the disputes generate ignorance,
in contrast with the more usual sequence where ignorance generates
debate. Three classes of people oppose the truth Dante wishes to
show: the pope and other prelates, whose motivation is their zealous
concern for the church and who are honest if misguided; a second
group, motivated by greed, who claim to be sons of the church yet
deny first principles, and with whom discussion would be futile;
and a third group, the decretalists, who regard the decretals (the
corpus of papal decrees and epistles which form the basis of ecclesiastical law) as the only authoritative source of enlightenment on this
question. They are entirely mistaken, for the decretals post-date the
church and therefore cannot be the source of its authority. Dante's
arguments are addressed only to the first group, who sincerely and
for the best of motives believe that the authority of the empire is
dependent on that of the church, and who are urged to accept Dante's arguments in the spirit in which they are offered, that of a
devout and dutiful son of the church who speaks out in the cause
of truth.

Of the six arguments based on scripture, three are from the Old
Testament and three from the New. The arguments are dealt with
in the order in which they occur in the Bible, rather than in the
order of their inherent forcefulness or their popularity among papal
supporters: this order, as we shall see, has certain advantages. Dante's refutations are precise and technical: in ch. iv he reminds us
both of the various kinds of refutation possible in syllogistic argument, as set out by Aristotle in the *Sophistical Refutations*, and of
the ways in which it is possible to misinterpret the mystical or
allegorical sense of scripture, as clarified by Augustine in the *De
civitate Dei* and the *De doctrina christiana*. Syllogistic arguments can
be unsound in form or in content; the logic may be faulty, or a
premiss untrue (either wholly false or false in some respect). Two
kinds of interpretative error can be made in relation to the allegorical sense: either looking for a mystical sense where there is none,
or interpreting in a way which misrepresents the intention of the

original writer or speaker. Armed with these methodological weapons, Dante now engages with the first group of arguments, all of which involve a tendentious interpretation of a scriptural passage from which inadmissible inferences are drawn.

The argument from the 'two great lights' spoken of in the first book of Genesis is that the sun and the moon allegorically represent spiritual and temporal power; the moon receives its light from the sun; therefore the empire receives its authority from the church. This was one of the oldest and most widely used of hierocratic arguments, and had become a commonplace of papal propaganda in the thirteenth and early fourteenth centuries, culminating in its use in both the *Allegacio* to Boniface VIII's *Unam sanctam*, and Clement V's letter to Henry VII. The hierocratic interpretation of Genesis is refuted by Dante on grounds of chronology (sun and moon were created on the fourth day, man on the sixth): it requires God to have created accidents before their subject (an absurdity) and a remedy before the condition which it is meant to correct (equally preposterous). (The Augustinian idea of the state as a *remedium peccati*, a consequence of man's Fall, is touched on but not developed; the possible conflict with the Aristotelian notion of the state as a natural construct, necessary because of human nature – the basis of the thesis developed in Book I – is not explored.) A less damning refutation can be made by drawing a distinction: the sun is not the source of the moon's existence or its light (i.e. its power), but it may cause the moon to operate more efficaciously; equally the pope is not the source or cause of the emperor's existence or power (i.e. his authority), but he may help the emperor function more effectively [*virtuosius*]. This suggestion that a cooperative and enriching relationship might be possible between papal and imperial authority sounds a moderate and conciliatory note at the end of this first refutation. It is an idea Dante will return to in the closing lines of the treatise.

The second argument (based on Genesis 29) takes the figures of Levi and Judah, the sons of Jacob, who were the father of the priesthood and the father of temporal rule respectively; they are held to prefigure the spiritual and temporal powers, the second being subordinate to the first as younger son is to older. Again there is a technical demonstration of the invalidity of the argument, which uses four terms instead of three, confusing seniority by birth with seniority in authority, and adducing the first to be the cause of the second, which clearly it is not.

The next argument is based on the account in Kings of the anointing and deposing of Saul by Samuel, God's vicar, who is shown there to have the power both to give and to take away temporal authority. Dante's refutation is based on the distinction between the roles of vicar and messenger. Samuel on this occasion functioned as God's messenger on an *ad hoc* mission to perform a specific task, not as a vicar in the sense in which the pope is God's vicar. No legitimate conclusion can be drawn from this episode about the powers of God's vicar.

The first of the scriptural arguments from the New Testament takes the story in Matthew of the offerings of the Magi at Christ's birth. The frankincense and gold are held to represent the spiritual and the temporal spheres in human life. Both were offered to Christ; Christ's vicar is thus lord and ruler over both. Again there is a formal error in the argument: the syllogism uses four terms instead of three. Christ and Christ's vicar are not interchangeable terms. This crucial distinction in a sense underlies the whole of Book III.

The last two arguments from biblical exegesis focus on a pair of texts whose significance had been expounded and debated for centuries to justify the supremacy of papal authority: Matthew 16, 19 and Luke 22, 38. These are Christ's words to Peter on handing him the keys: 'Whatsoever thou shalt bind on earth shall be bound in heaven; and whatsoever thou shalt loose on earth shall be loosed in heaven. . .'; and Peter's words to Christ: 'Behold, here are two swords.' Dante's treatment of these two key Petrine texts takes us to the heart of papal claims for power in temporal affairs and occupies the very centre of Book III.

The power of binding and loosing conferred by Christ on Peter is taken by papal apologists to include the laws and decrees of empire. Once again Dante points to a technical error in their argument. The exact scope of the word 'whatsoever' is delimited by what it refers to: the word was not used by Christ in an absolute sense, but in relation to something quite specific, namely Peter's role as keeper of the keys. If Peter's powers to bind and loose were unlimited, as is claimed, he would have the power to do things which he clearly cannot do, like divorcing husband from wife and forgiving the unrepentant. (A whole section of the *Summule – De distributionibus* – deals with just this issue, the need for meticulous care in interpreting universals and their range of reference. With a simple argument from logic Dante cuts through a centuries-long tradition of legalistic debate and commentary.)

The swords of which Peter speaks when he says to Christ 'Behold, here are two swords' were taken by papal supporters to represent the two powers, which (they allege) are here clearly identified as belonging to Peter. The allegorical interpretation which equates the two swords with the two powers must be rejected, Dante argues, and for two reasons. (By questioning the validity of the initial assumption he again cuts straight to the heart of his opponents' case.) It is at odds with Christ's intention when he first spoke of the swords, for he clearly meant that the disciples should have one sword each; and it is incompatible with Peter's simple and ingenuous nature and his well-documented habit of answering impulsively and unreflectingly, in a way which precludes any deeper meaning. A long list of examples engagingly illustrates this propensity: it would have been quite out of character for Peter to answer with the intention the papal supporters claim. Dante's rebuttal finishes with a counter argument: if the swords are to be interpreted figuratively, it is in a quite different sense, with reference to the sword mentioned by Christ in Matthew: 'I came not to send peace, but a sword. . .'. On this view the swords would represent a willingness to engage actively with the world to spread the Christian message by word and deed – an allegorical interpretation for which scholars have not identified a source and which appears to be Dante's own.

Dante has given a dazzling display of his command of formal logic and its procedures, demolishing his opponents' arguments by demonstrating that they embody a series of identifiable fallacies: the *fallacia accidentis*, the *fallacia secundum non causam ut causam*, the *fallacia secundum quid et simpliciter*, the error of false distribution, the formal error of using four terms instead of the mandatory three in a syllogism. Equally remarkable is his boldness of attack in handling biblical interpretation, reflecting a confident familiarity with the Bible and a sense of real intimacy with biblical figures, whose intentions and personality he assesses with complete self-assurance.

Dante's demolition of the six arguments based on 'the word of God' serves as a preliminary clearing of the ground; he is now ready to tackle the thorniest issue of all, the arguments based on history. The first of these concerns the so-called 'donation of Constantine', the gift supposedly made to pope Sylvester by the emperor Constantine – out of gratitude for his miraculous cure from leprosy and as a sign of his conversion to the Christian faith – of territory which included the city of Rome and of many imperial prerogatives and privileges. Since that time, the argument runs, these things have belonged to the church and been subject to the church's authority. The document which records this gift is spurious, but Dante like most of his contemporaries believed it to be genuine, and believed the 'donation' itself to be a matter of historical fact. His argument is concerned with its validity in a far more profound sense: was an emperor entitled to do what Constantine did? Dante argues that Constantine was not in a position to give away imperial territory or privileges, nor was the church in a position to accept them. His action was in conflict with the nature of imperial office, which is by definition – the whole of Books I and II have demonstrated this – a single and indivisible rule over the whole human race. The foundation of empire is human right; the emperor must therefore not do anything in conflict with human right; but human right requires an undivided worldwide empire; to divide that empire is to destroy it. The emperor cannot destroy the very thing which makes him what he is: his being and function are defined precisely in terms of universality. Equally, the church is unsuited to receiving temporal assets, in accordance with Christ's express injunction ('Provide neither gold, nor silver, nor brass in your purses. . .') as recorded by the evangelists. All that could be legitimately done by an emperor is the consigning of a patrimony into the guardianship of the church, for the benefit of the poor. Constantine's action was well-meaning, but it undermined and called into question the very nature of empire and imperial authority.

There is a second argument from history, but it is summarily dismissed. Charlemagne was crowned emperor by pope Hadrian, who called on him for protection against the incursions of the Longobards; since that time emperors are legitimately considered to be defenders of the church and subject to the church's authority. But,

Dante counters, the usurpation of a right does not establish a right. If it did, then the contrary case could be argued with equal force, for the emperor Otto restored pope Leo to power when he had been displaced by Benedict, suggesting that papal office and authority were in the gift of the emperor. The terseness of Dante's rebuttal is striking, for the *translatio imperii* was one of the principal arguments used by the hierocrats as confirmation of papal possession of both swords, and the juridical significance of papal coronation of an emperor had been a focus of debate for centuries.

The last of the arguments used by the papal apologists is the argument from reason, which draws on the Aristotelian principle of *reductio ad unum*, i.e. the principle that all things belonging to one species are referable to a single entity which is the measure or exemplar for all members of the species. In the case of men, this must be to a man. The pope cannot be referred to any other man, so he must be the one to whom all others, including the emperor, are referred. But this argument too commits the accidental fallacy, i.e. it confuses accident with substance. Again it is logic which enables Dante to cut through obfuscation to a simple truth. Pope and emperor are what they are by virtue of their relationships to other people, which are relationships of authority, whereas man is a substance, defined in terms of his essential nature. As men, they are referred to a single man; as pope and emperor, they are referred not to a person, but to the principle of authority: either God himself, or some lower principle of authority emanating from him. *Reductio ad unum* has been described as the fundamental imperative of medieval culture; the whole of Book I of the *Monarchia* could be seen as a working out of this principle. Here Dante dismisses the hierocratic version of the same argument, which misapplies the principle by using faulty logic. Having disposed of it, he is ready to develop his own arguments in support of imperial independence of papal authority, which occupy the final chapters of the treatise.

The first of these is the chronological argument: the empire functioned with all its power and authority before the church existed. The church *cannot* therefore be the source of that power and authority. The second concerns the source of the church's alleged temporal power. This power does not come from God (whether from natural law or divine law); nor can it have come from the church itself (a logical impossibility); nor did it come from the empire, as we have seen in relation to Constantine; nor did it come from mankind as a whole, or the majority of mankind (Asians and Africans and even most Europeans do not acknowledge the church's authority). There is no identifiable source for this alleged power of the church, which does not, in fact, exist.

The most important argument Dante saves until last. If the church had power over temporal concerns, this would be in conflict with its very nature. Christ's life is a model for the church, its pastors and the pope. But Christ himself specifically renounced the kingdom of this world, as the Bible makes unequivocally clear; the church would be in conflict with its own nature if it were to do otherwise. The principle enunciated at the beginning of Book III is thus doubly negated or violated by the hierocratic case: it is against nature's intention that the empire should be divided, just as it is against nature's intention that the church should exercise power *in temporalibus*.

Dante's last chapter offers a final 'positive' proof that the emperor's authority comes to him directly from God and not from an intermediary. We come full circle to our starting-point, the fact of man's double nature, the combination in human beings of body and mind, corruptible and incorruptible. Every nature has its own 'final end' or ultimate goal. Mankind, having two natures, must necessarily have two such goals. These are the happiness of this life and the happiness of the eternal life, signified respectively by the earthly and the heavenly paradise. These goals are achieved by different means: on the one hand, the teachings of philosophy and the exercise of the moral and intellectual virtues; on the other, spiritual teachings and the practice of the theological virtues of faith, hope and charity. Humanity needs two guides corresponding to these two goals: emperor and pope. We are reminded for the last time of the need for peace if human beings are to find fulfilment, and of the function of the emperor as a guarantor of peace and freedom. We are reminded too of the reflection of the cosmic order in the ordering of our human world. The point made so powerfully at the very centre of the treatise – humanity's purpose seen as a part of nature's broader purpose – is now linked to the creator of both the human and the natural order. Only God takes in the cosmic order at a glance. He alone therefore can make provision for the emperor. God alone chooses, he alone confirms. The so-called 'electors' to imperial office – the college of German princes responsible for choosing the emperor – are no more than mouthpieces of divine providence. It is inevitable that there will be occasional disagreements among them, for some will perceive God's will less clearly than others, and some not at all. There is a direct line of authority, with no intermediary, from God the Fountainhead of universal authority to the emperor, which parallels and is distinct from the direct line of authority from God to the pope.

The task is now complete. The three points of inquiry have been clarified and resolved. We have seen that the well-being of the world requires a supreme world-ruler set over all lesser kings and princes; that the rise to power of the Roman empire was a part of God's providential plan for humanity; and that the emperor's authority, which comes to him directly from God, is independent of the pope. But in his final paragraph Dante adds a coda which has caused some perplexity – the emperor is 'in some respect' [*in aliquo*] subject to the pope, just as earthly happiness is 'in some sense' [*quodammodo*] ordered to immortal happiness. Let the emperor treat the pope with the respect and reverence a first-born son owes his father, so that he may the better [*virtuosius*] light up the world with his guidance and example. The positive relationship between the two powers first hinted at as Dante embarked on his demolition of the case for papal supremacy in temporal affairs in III, iv is echoed here: the spirit of cooperation and reconciliation there adumbrated is urged again in Dante's concluding sentence, whose final words, however, remind us of God's role as the only source of both imperial and papal power.

The text we have just described is equally remarkable as an argument and as an artefact. The richness and originality of the arguments Dante uses to defend his thesis are matched by the intellectual rigour with which they are developed, and the incisiveness and energy with which the debate is conducted. But equally striking, on reflection, is the sense the treatise gives of being a carefully constructed whole, where formal considerations relating to how the material is organized – considerations of symmetry and balance, of sequence and order – play an important part. We have noted the parallels between the three books, both in the laying out of the argument and in the framing effect of the opening and closing chapters – chapters noticeable both for their density of scriptural allusion, and for their insistent use of the *cursus* or rhythmical patterning of the prose to produce an effect of rhetorical heightening. We have noted too how in each book the most important argument is placed right at the centre, physical centrality reflecting intellectual weight and cogency. As I have argued elsewhere, the symmetries and patterning detectable in the treatise may have been planned by Dante around a numerical model,[6] the mathematical shaping and ordering principles which underlie reality itself built into the very structure of the text. Certainly the three-in-one structure of the *Monarchy* (three books, one treatise) satisfyingly echoes not only the structure of the Trinity but also that of the syllogism (three terms, one argument; three propositions, one conclusion). Indeed the *Monarchy* itself can be seen as a kind of syllogism, the conclusion of Book III being the inevitable consequence of acknowledging the truth of the propositions advanced in Books I and II.

Although each book is self-contained, there are thematic links and echoes from book to book, recurring motifs which create a powerfully unifying effect. The donation of Constantine, on which Dante focuses with the full force of reasoned argument only in III, x, is alluded to in Books I and II, each of which in its concluding chapter had a veiled allusion to the destructive folly of the emperor's action – equated in I, xvi with the rending of Christ's seamless garment and identified in II, xi as the source of all of Italy's present misfortunes. *Iustitia* – justice or, in the language of the Authorized Version, righteousness – is a recurring theme: it is the supreme good in human affairs, in terms of which the emperor's function can be defined; it is a key to understanding certain aspects of Roman history; it is the measure of the church's corruption, for the church makes only a pretence of justice; Dante's concern for justice identifies him as the heir to Daniel and to David. The most insistent and powerful of all these recurring themes is *cupiditas*, which signifies both the desire for self-enrichment and the *libido dominandi*, and which is condemned for its damaging and divisive effects on society and political organization. It prevents lesser rulers from achieving peace and stability; it was repudiated by the great Romans whose lives were lived by the ideals of selflessness and

---

[6] See the Introduction to the Cambridge Medieval Classics edition of the text, pp. xxxvi–xxxvii.

austerity; it prevents Dante's opponents from acknowledging the force of his arguments, since it blinds them to first principles. On the opening page of the treatise, it is the reason this subject has been neglected by other writers, for it will not lead to wealth or material advantage. On the closing page it is identified once again as the reason the world will always need an emperor. The simplicity and power of Dante's vision of a political order which could curb and direct the impulses of frail humanity towards an achievable goal of human fulfilment and happiness comes from a profoundly ethical basis.

Another linking or unifying principle in the *Monarchy* is its intertextuality. When confronted with the richness and variety of Dante's allusions to other writers and other works – the omnipresence of Aristotle and (in Book II) of Virgil, and alongside them the many lesser yet still great figures such as Lucan, Livy, Cicero, Orosius, Boethius, Aquinas and Augustine – it is easy to overlook the fact that the Bible is textually represented in the *Monarchy* with extraordinary fullness and completeness. (One of the paradoxes the treatise confronts us with is that a writer so steeped in the works of others, and so acutely conscious of and eager to acknowledge his indebtedness, can have produced a work of such startling originality.) The Psalms alone are cited more often than Aristotle's *Politics*; each of the five books of the Pentateuch is quoted or referred to explicitly, as are all of St Paul's major epistles (to the Romans, Corinthians, Galatians, Ephesians, Philippians, Colossians, Thessalonians, Timothy and Hebrews); the Gospels, of course, are everywhere. It can hardly be doubted that this was a deliberate authorial strategy. In the extraordinarily rich intellectual humus out of which the *Monarchy* grows and to which Dante explicitly pays tribute, the most important authority of all remains the Bible. And it is the words of Christ himself which stand at the centre of Dante's political philosophy and which guarantee the conclusions of Book III: Take no gold or silver...My kingdom is not of this world...Peter, follow me.

Dante's treatise, so often described by later historians as backward-looking and hopelessly unrealistic as a solution to the problems of his age – an age when the restoration of an empire was becoming an increasingly remote likelihood as perceptions of national identity and state boundaries were hardening – was nonetheless judged sufficiently dangerous by his immediate and near contemporaries to merit a detailed rebuttal by a Dominican friar (*c.* 1327), a ritual burning on the orders of a higher prelate in 1329, only a few years after Dante's death, and, in the fullness of time, a place on the Vatican's Index of prohibited books (1554). On the positive side, it inspired Cola di Rienzo to write a commentary, and Marsilio Ficino to make a translation (probably out of frustration with an earlier anonymous version which obscured rather than clarified Dante's meaning). It was first printed at Basle (a centre of activity for the Reformation) in 1559, just five years after being placed on the Index – where it remained until as recently as 1881.

Many scholars, perhaps most, have preferred a dating for the *Monarchia* which links it closely to historical circumstances – to the period of the newly elected Emperor Henry VII's descent into Italy or the years close to it, and to the letters Dante wrote at this time (1310–11) urging the emperor to come and urging Italians to welcome him. (When Henry's expedition, of which Dante had such high hopes, failed, the cause was once again the recalcitrance of the Florentines and the duplicity of a pope, Clement V.) But the points of resemblance between the treatise and the letters Dante wrote at the time of Henry's Italian expedition are no more striking than the differences between them. There are differences in method and above all in tone: rousing exhortation and a dramatic sense of the immediacy of events in the letters, calm and objective philosophical analysis in the treatise. In the *Monarchy*, as Etienne Gilson succinctly put it, Dante is not fighting for a man, but for an idea.[7]

A later dating for the treatise (certainly no earlier than 1314, and possibly the very last years of its author's life) is imposed by the cross-reference in Book I to the *Paradiso*, a cross-reference whose authenticity has been repeatedly called into question, but which there seems no good reason to doubt.[8] In terms of psychology it seems at least as plausible that Dante would compose a treatise demonstrating the need for an emperor when his hopes in practical terms of ever seeing this come about in his own lifetime had been definitively dashed. The opening sentence of the treatise makes it

---

[7] E. Gilson, *Dante et la philosophie* , second edn, Paris 1953, p. 173. (English translation: *Dante the Philosopher*, translated by D. Moore, London 1948, p. 172.)
[8] A fuller account of the scholarly debate is given in the Introduction to the Cambridge Medieval Classics edition of the *Monarchia*, pp. xxxviii–xli.

incontrovertibly clear that he is writing with his eye on and for the benefit of posterity. This is his legacy to the world: a philosophical demonstration of the way humanity ought to be ordered politically as a collectivity, to stand alongside his poetic masterpiece, the *Divine Comedy*, which shows individuals how to achieve salvation. The two visions are inextricably linked, and there is much overlapping of material between them. There is no conflict at all between poem and treatise in what Dante advocated in terms of practical politics: the separation of secular from ecclesiastical power, and a return to apostolic poverty for the church, whose greed and manifest corruption were the cause of Italy's turbulence and lawlessness. It does not seem too wide of the mark to suggest that the *Monarchy* stands in relation to the *Comedy* as Aristotle's *Politics* stands in relation to his *Ethics* – a text which grows out of an earlier one, clarifying and developing one aspect of it, introducing new emphases which some commentators have found problematical, but a product of the same searching and tirelessly creative mind whose primary concern was always doing and making [*agere et facere*] rather than theory: 'the present subject is not directed primarily towards theoretical understanding but towards action' [*materia presens non ad speculationem per prius, sed ad operationem ordinatur*]. Compressed, bitter, spare, energetic and beautifully crafted, it bears the unmistakable imprint of his genius.

Editor's note

The translation

The difficulties posed by translating a text like the *Monarchy* are considerable. Dante's language is concise and vigorous, yet dense with philosophical implications: to find a balance between literal translation and explanatory paraphrase is a constant challenge. I have tried to keep as close to the original text as seemed consistent with modern English usage, preferring to clarify in notes rather than to stray too far from Dante's formulations, and avoiding (I hope) the ponderousness (and even occasional opacity) of some earlier versions, qualities which seem to me entirely alien to Dante's style.

The translation is based on the Latin text printed in the Cambridge Medieval Classics edition of the *Monarchia*, which in its turn is based on the text established by Pier Giorgio Ricci in his 1965 edition of the treatise,[1] emended in some forty odd places. Most of these emendations do not affect the meaning: a small group of substantive changes (concentrated at the end of Book II, chapter x) is described in 'Some proposed emendations to the text of Dante's *Monarchia*', in *Italian Studies* 50, 1995, pp. 1–8. Where Ricci's text diverges from Rostagno's earlier edition (see Bibliographical note), the present translation will differ from earlier English versions. The critical edition of the Latin text of the *Monarchy* which I am cur-

---

[1] Dante Alighieri, *Monarchia, a cura di* P. G. Ricci (Edizione Nazionale delle opere di Dante Alighieri a cura della Societá Dantesca Italiana, vol. v), Milano 1965 (henceforth in the notes *EN*).

rently preparing, and which will be published under the auspices of the Società Dantesca Italiana, will include a full critical apparatus and an exhaustive discussion of the textual situation.

I have chosen to cite the Bible in the Authorized Version (henceforth AV), because it seems important that biblical quotations in the text, even when not identified as such by Dante, should be instantly recognizable. While it is true that the distance between the language of the AV and modern English is greater than that between Dante's Latin and the Latin of the Vulgate, there can be no doubt that Dante could count on his readers' recognition of the biblical source in a way that we no longer can. Where the English of the AV does not correspond to the Latin quoted by Dante, or blurs the development of his argument, or cannot be accommodated syntactically, the translation is my own. The lines from Boethius on p. 53 are from V. E. Watts's version of *The Consolation of Philosophy*, Reading 1969 (by kind permission of Penguin Books Ltd). The translation of all other authors cited by Dante is my own.

The notes

The notes for this edition of the *Monarchy* are a leaner version of those which appear in the Cambridge Medieval Latin Classics volume *Monarchia*, where the English text stands alongside the Latin original. Certain categories of note have been eliminated altogether: cross-references to other works by Dante; references to textual problems; alternative interpretations of particular words or phrases; and, to a large extent, references to the commentaries of other scholars (most notably Gustavo Vinay and Bruno Nardi),[2] to whom, in the fuller version, my indebtedness is everywhere apparent. Readers interested in any or all of these questions are urged to consult the fuller version, also published by the Cambridge University Press.

The notes as they now stand in this volume:

(a) give precise references for texts quoted by Dante;
(b) gloss words or phrases which can be elucidated by cross-reference to the *Monarchy*;

---

[2] See Bibliographical note.

(c) clarify the structure and articulation of the argument (a source of particular difficulty for readers not familiar with syllogistic reasoning);

(d) indicate how Dante's political theory connects with his 'world view'. For those wishing to ground their understanding of Dante's political ideas in a broader understanding of his philosophy and science, the two volumes by Patrick Boyde cited in the Bibliographical note are invaluable, and are repeatedly indicated as a point of departure.

For uniformity and ease of reference, Aristotle is cited in the notes from *The Complete Works of Aristotle, The Revised Oxford Translation*, edited by Jonathan Barnes, Princeton 1981. (Chapter numbers will occasionally differ from those cited by Italian scholars.) *Ethics* refers always, in text and notes, to the *Nicomachean Ethics*; Aquinas' commentary on this work is referred to in the notes in the abbreviated form Aquinas *In Eth.* Translations from Orosius in the notes are by I. W. Raymond, *Seven Books of History Against the Pagans*, New York 1936. The translations from St Augustine in the Introduction are from *The City of God*, vol. I, translated by Demetrius B. Zenia, S. J. and Gerald G. Walsh, S. J., Washington 1962 (by kind permission of the Catholic University Press of America).

The titles of works by authors other than Dante are given in full on the first occasion on which they are cited; subsequent references to the same work will give the author's name only or, where this would be ambiguous, the author's name and a short form of the title. The *Monarchy* itself is referred to in the notes in the abbreviated form *Mon.*

Principal events in Dante's life

1250   Death of Emperor Frederick II; for 60 years there will be no crowned Holy Roman Emperor, and there will be no effective incumbent in Dante's lifetime.

1265   Dante is born in Florence.

        c. 1283→ Dante establishes himself as a leading love poet in Florence.

1289   Battle of Campaldino, in which Dante serves with the Florentine Guelf forces against the Ghibelline city of Arezzo.

        c. 1292 Dante assembles an anthology of his poems with linking narrative to form the *Vita nuova.*

        c. 1293 → Dante embarks on the study of philosophy; he goes on to write poems on philosophical themes.

1294   Boniface VIII becomes Pope.

1295   Dante enters political life in the commune of Florence, having enrolled in the guild of physicians and apothecaries; in the following years he serves on several councils; the Guelfs split into two factions, which will become known as Blacks and Whites.

1300   15 *June* – 15 *August*: Dante serves as one of the six priors who exercise executive power under the Gonfaloniere di Giustizia.

   1300 *Easter*: the fictional date of Dante's journey to the realms of the afterlife as it will be described in the *Comedy*.

1301   *October*: Dante is absent from Florence when the Black Guelfs, whose leaders had recently been exiled, stage a coup and return to power (he is probably on a mission representing the commune at the papal curia in Rome).

1302   27 *January*: in his absence Dante is fined, excluded from public office and banished from Tuscany on a fabricated charge of corruption.
   10 *March*: the sentence is confirmed; if Dante falls into the commune's power he will be burnt at the stake.
   December: Boniface proclaims the supreme authority of the church in temporal affairs in the bull *Unam sanctam*.

1303   *October*: Death of Boniface.
   Election of Benedict XI, who dies the following year.

1304   Dante becomes a 'party on his own', abandoning his allegiance to his fellow White Guelf exiles; in the following years, he travels extensively all over Italy.

   c. 1304–*c.* 1308 Dante writes the *De vulgari eloquentia* and the *Convivio*, which is to provide an extensive prose commentary on his philosophical poems (both works remain unfinished); in *Convivio* IV, iii–vi, he sets out a first version of some of the arguments he will use in the *Monarchy*.

1305   Election of Pope Clement V, a Frenchman who never comes to Rome; the Papacy is subsequently established in Avignon.

1308   Henry of Luxembourg is chosen by the imperial Electors, and has Clement's backing.

   c. 1308 Dante starts the *Comedy*, which he works on until shortly before his death.

1309 *January*: Henry is crowned as Emperor Henry VII at Aix-la-Chapelle.

1310 *October*: Henry VII embarks on his Italian campaign. Dante writes an open letter in Latin to the rulers and people of Italy, urging them to welcome the emperor, who will bring peace and justice.

1311 *January*: Henry VII is crowned in Milan.
31 *March*: Dante writes to the Florentines, urging them to recognize Henry.
17 *April*: Dante writes to the Emperor, urging him to act against Florence, 'the viper that turns against the vitals of her mother'.

1312 *June*: Henry VII is crowned in Rome, but (because of Papal opposition) not in St Peter's.

1313 *April*: Henry declares all men subject to the Emperor's authority.
June: Clement's bull *Pastoralis cura* rejects imperial claims to overlordship.
August: Henry VII dies; the imperial Electors fail to reach agreement on a successor.

  1314 At the very earliest and possibly much later, Dante writes the *Monarchy*.

1315 *June*: an amnesty is offered to the Florentine exiles, provided they acknowledge their guilt; Dante rejects the offer.
October: Dante's exile from Florence is reconfirmed for life and is now extended to his children (his punishment if captured will be decapitation); his later years are spent at Verona at the court of Can Grande della Scala and at Ravenna at the court of Guido Novello da Polenta.

  c. 1320 Dante writes the *Questio* and the *Egloge*.

1321 Dante dies at Ravenna.
  c. 1327 Guido Vernani writes the *De reprobatione Monarchiae*.

1329   According to Boccaccio, the *Monarchy* is publicly burnt as a heretical text in Bologna, but a plan to burn Dante's bones with his treatise is foiled.

1554   The *Monarchy* is placed on the Vatican's Index of prohibited books, from which it is removed only in 1881.

1559   The *editio princeps* is published in Basle.

Bibliographical note

The two most commonly cited editions of the Latin text of Dante's treatise are those of Rostagno and Ricci: Dante Alighieri, *Monarchia, a cura di* E. Rostagno, in Le Opere di Dante. Testo critico della Società Dantesca Italiana, Firenze 1921, second edn 1960; and Dante Alighieri, *Monarchia, a cura di* P. G. Ricci (Edizione Nazionale delle opere di Dante Alighieri a cura della Società Dantesca Italiana, vol. v), Milano 1965. There are significant differences between the two, Ricci's text representing an improvement on Rostagno's in a score of places. (A new critical edition of the Latin text by the translator and editor of this volume is at an advanced stage of preparation.) The English versions of the *Monarchy* most widely quoted are those of Wicksteed and Nicholl: P. H. Wicksteed, *The De Monarchia*, Hull 1896 (subsequently reprinted in the Temple Classics series); and Dante, *Monarchy and Three Political Letters*, with an introduction by Donald Nicholl, London 1954. The second represents a notable improvement on the first in terms of readability, but is not without inaccuracies, omissions and (inevitably, given that it is based on Rostagno's Latin text) renderings which do not correspond to an up-to-date Latin text. Dante's *Convivio*, which in its fourth book rehearses some of the arguments on empire that Dante will develop in the *Monarchy*, is now available in a good new English version: Dante, *The Banquet*, translated by C. Ryan, Saratoga, California, 1989.

Excellent brief accounts of Dante's life, including his political career up to the time of his exile, are to be found in G. Padoan, *Introduzione a Dante*, Firenze 1975; R. Migliorini Fissi, *Dante*, Firenze 1979; and G. Holmes, *Dante*, Oxford 1980. A magisterial survey of Dante's political activity and thinking throughout his life is given by F. Mazzoni, 'Teoresi e prassi in Dante politico', the introductory essay in the volume Dante Alighieri, *Monarchia. Epistole Politiche*, Edizioni Rai Italiane, Torino 1966. All three Italian scholars give extensive bibliographical references. The archival material which enables us to document Dante's political career is collected in the *Codice diplomatico dantesco, edito da* R. Piattoli, Firenze 1940.

A first point of departure for those wishing to investigate the sources of Dante's political ideas must be the magisterial commentaries on the *Monarchy* by Gustavo Vinay and Bruno Nardi, with their abundant citations of source material, especially from medieval commentaries on Aristotle: Dante Alighieri, *Monarchia. Testo introduzione traduzione e commento, a cura di* Gustavo Vinay, Firenze 1950; Dante Alighieri, *Monarchia, a cura di* Bruno Nardi, in *Opere Minori*, Tomo II, Milano-Napoli 1979. The more recent annotated edition of Maurizio Pizzica is very useful in updating some of their conclusions, and contains a valuable introductory essay placing Dante's treatise against the background of earlier and contemporary political debate: Dante Alighieri, *Monarchia, a cura di* Maurizio Pizzica, Milano 1988. An English commentary by Professor Richard Kay of the University of Kansas is in an advanced state of preparation.

General reference works of great usefulness are *A Dictionary of Proper Names and Notable Matters in the Works of Dante*, by Paget Toynbee, revised by Charles Singleton, Oxford 1968; and the invaluable *Enciclopedia dantesca* (hereafter *ED*) I–VI, Rome 1970–8, which contains articles by scholars of international standing on all aspects of Dante's life, thought and work.

Two excellent brief introductions to the philosophy of Aristotle are J. L. Ackrill's *Aristotle the Philosopher*, Oxford 1981 and J. Barnes's *Aristotle*, Oxford 1982. *The Cambridge Companion to Aristotle*, edited by J. Barnes, Cambridge 1995, is a collection of essays on different aspects of the philosopher's work (R. Smith's 'Logic' being especially helpful to a student of the *Monarchy*). Two volumes by P. Boyde together form an authoritative, lucid, and comprehensive exposition of Dante's understanding of Aristotle's thought: *Dante Philomythes and Philosopher. Man in the Cosmos*, Cambridge 1981 (cosmology, physics, astronomy and biology), and *Perception and Passion in Dante's Comedy*, Cambridge 1993 (human physiology and psychology). Two studies more narrowly focused on Dante and the *Politics* are A. H. Gilbert, 'Had Dante read the *Politics* of Aristotle?' in *Publications of the Modern Languages Association* 43, 1928, pp. 602–13; and L. Minio-Paluello, 'Dante's Reading of Aristotle', in *The World of Dante. Essays on Dante and his Times*, edited by C. Grayson, Oxford 1980, pp. 61–80. The article by E. Berti, 'Politica' (i.e. Aristotle's *Politics*), in *ED* IV, pp. 585–7, gives a useful overview.

D. Comparetti's *Vergil in the Middle Ages*, translated by E. F. M. Benecke, London 1895, remains the classic scholarly account of perceptions of Virgil in the Middle Ages, and includes a chapter on Dante. An excellent introduction to Virgil and his poem is K. W. Gransden's *The Aeneid*, Cambridge 1990. R. Fitzgerald's superb verse translation of the *Aeneid* is now available in the Penguin Classics.

On Dante and the Bible the following are useful: E. Moore, *Studies in Dante. First Series. Scripture and Classical Authors in Dante.* Oxford 1896 (lithographic reprint 1969); Peter S. Hawkins, 'Dante and the Bible', in *The Cambridge Companion to Dante*, edited by Rachel Jacoff, Cambridge 1993, pp. 120–35; and C. Vasoli, 'La Bibbia nel *Convivio* e nella *Monarchia*', in *Dante e la Bibbia, a cura di* G. Barblan, Firenze 1988, pp. 19–39.

Aquinas' commentary on Aristotle's *Ethics*, a text of fundamental importance for understanding Dante, is available in English: Sancti Thomae Aquinatis *In decem libros Ethicorum Aristotelis ad Nicomachum Expositio*, Editio tertia, cura et studio P. Fr. Raymundi M. Spiazzi O.P., Turin 1964 (English translation by C. I. Litzinger, Chicago 1964); so too is the commentary on the *De anima*: Sancti Thomae Aquinatis *In Aristotelis librum De anima Commentarium*, Editio quinta, cura ac studio P. F. Angeli M. Pirotta, O.P., Turin 1959 (English translation: *Aristotle's De anima in the Version of William of Moerbeke and the Commentary of St Thomas Aquinas*, translated by Kenelm Foster, O.P., M.A. and Silvester Humphries, O.P., M.A. with an Introduction by Ivo Thomas, O.P., M.A., London 1951). The commentary on the *Politics* is also of interest: S. Thomae Aquinatis *In octo libros Politicorum Aristotelis Expositio*, Cura et studio P. Fr. Raymundi M. Spiazzi O.P., Turin 1966.

English versions of some of Dante's more important medieval precursors and sources are: St Thomas Aquinas, *On Kingship to the King of Cyprus*, done into English by G. B. Phelan (under the title *On the Governance of Rulers*), revised with introduction and notes by I. Th. Eschmann O.P., Toronto 1949; St Thomas Aquinas, *Summa contra Gentiles, Book III: Providence*, translated, with an introduction and notes, by Vernon J. Bourke, Notre Dame 1975; St Thomas Aquinas, *Summa theologiae*, Latin text and English translation, introductions, notes, appendices and glossaries, ed. Thomas Gilbert and T. C. O'Brien, London and New York, 1964–80, especially vol. 28: *Law and Political Theory*; St Augustine, *The City of God*, translated by Demetrius B. Zenia, S. J. and Gerald G. Walsh, S. J., Washington 1962; St Augustine, *On Christian Doctrine* (*De doctrina christiana*), translated, with an introduction, by D. W. Robertson, Indianapolis 1958; Boethius, *The Consolation of Philosophy*, translated with an introduction by V. E. Watts, Reading 1969; Paulus Orosius, *Seven Books of History Against the Pagans*, translated by I. W. Raymond, New York 1936. On these and other figures the *ED* entries are excellent; particular attention should perhaps be drawn to C. Vasoli, 'Averroè', in *ED* I, pp. 473–9, and the same scholar's 'intelletto possibile', in *ED* III, pp. 469–72.

On Aristotelian logic as practised by the scholastics and by Dante, the indispensable basic text is Peter of Spain, *Tractatus called afterwards Summule logicales*, ed. by L. M. De Rijk, Assen 1972. An earlier edition, Petri Hispani *Summulae logicales*, a cura di I. M. Bocheński O. P., Torino 1947, is still useful, but is less reliable because less complete. Also pertinent is S. Thomae Aquinatis 'De fallaciis', in *Opuscula Omnia necnon Opera Minora. Tomus Primus. Opuscula philosophica*, ed. R. P. Joannes Perrier, O.P., Paris 1949, pp. 430–60. G. H. Joyce's *Principles of Logic*, third edn, London 1920, gives an extremely thorough exposition of the principles of Aristotelian formal logic as developed by the scholastics.

In addition to the fundamental essay by F. Mazzoni already mentioned, Dante's political thinking is dealt with in the following works: A. P. d'Entrèves, *Dante as a Political Thinker*, Oxford 1952; G. Holmes, 'Dante and the Popes', in *The World of Dante. Essays on Dante and his Times*, edited by C. Grayson, Oxford 1980, pp. 18–43; U. Limentani, 'Dante's Political Thought', in *The Mind of Dante*, edited by U. Limentani, Cambridge 1965, pp. 113–37; B.

Nardi, 'Tre pretese fasi del pensiero politico di Dante', in *Saggi di filosofia dantesca*, Milano 1930, pp. 307–45.

On the question of Dante's attitude to empire the classic scholarly study is C. T. Davis, *Dante and the Idea of Rome*, Oxford 1957; two more recent essays by the same author update his conclusions: 'Dante's Vision of History', in *Dante's Italy and Other Essays*, Philadelphia 1984, pp. 23–41; and 'Dante and the Empire', in *The Cambridge Companion to Dante*, edited by Rachel Jacoff, Cambridge 1993, pp. 67–79. Fundamental contributions by Italian scholars are M. Maccarrone, 'Papato e Impero nella "Monarchia" ', in *Nuove letture dantesche*, Firenze 1976, pp. 259–352; B. Nardi, 'Il concetto dell'Impero nello svolgimento del pensiero dantesco', in *Saggi di filosofia dantesca*, Milano 1930, pp. 239–305; P. G. Ricci, 'Dante e l'Impero di Roma', in *Dante e Roma. Atti del Convegno di Studi*, Firenze 1965, pp. 137–49.

Among the very many important critical and scholarly works on the *Monarchy* the following can be recommended as outstanding: A. M. Chiavacci Leonardi, 'La "Monarchia" di Dante alla luce della "Commedia" ', in *Studi medievali* 18, 1977, pp. 147–83; E. Gilson, *Dante et la philosophie* (ch. III: 'La Philosophie dans la "Monarchie" '), second edition, Paris 1953, pp. 163–222 (English translation: *Dante the Philosopher*, translated by D. Moore, London 1948); B. Nardi, 'Filosofia e teologia ai tempi di Dante', in *Saggi e note di critica dantesca*, Milano–Napoli 1966, pp. 3–109 (esp. pp. 56–73); B. Nardi, 'Dal "Convivio" alla "Commedia" ', in *Dal 'Convivio' alla 'Commedia'*, Roma 1960, pp. 37–150; V. Russo, 'La "Monarchia" di Dante (tra utopia e progetto)', in *Letture classensi* 7, Ravenna 1979, pp. 51–89; A. Vallone, *Dante* (ch. 7: 'La "Monarchia", l' "Epistole" politiche e il pensiero politico'), Milano 1971, pp. 173–236; C. Vasoli, 'Filosofia e teologia in Dante', in *Dante nella critica d'oggi* (*Cultura e Scuola* 4, 13–14), 1965, pp. 47–71; C. Vasoli, 'Filosofia e politica in Dante fra "Convivio" e "Monarchia" ', in *Letture classensi* 9–10, Ravenna 1982, pp. 11–37; G. Vinay, *Interpretazione della 'Monarchia' di Dante*, Firenze 1962.

Critical and scholarly works on particular aspects of the treatise include the following: C. T. Davis, 'Remigio de' Girolami and Dante: A Comparison of their Conceptions of Peace', in *Studi danteschi* 36, 1959, pp. 105–36; P. Fiorelli, 'Sul senso del diritto nella "Monarchia" ', in *Letture classensi* 16, Ravenna 1987, pp. 79–97; M.

Maccarrone, 'Il terzo libro della "Monarchia" ', in *Studi danteschi* 33, 1955, pp. 5–142; B. Nardi, 'Intorno ad una nuova inter-pretazione del terzo libro della *Monarchia* dantesca', in *Dal 'Convi-vio' alla 'Commedia'*, Roma 1960, pp. 151–313 (Nardi's response to Maccarrone's article); B. Nardi, 'La "Donatio Constantini" e Dante', in *Studi danteschi* 26, 1942, pp. 47–95 (reprinted in *Nel Mondo di Dante*, Roma 1944, pp. 109–59).

The best starting-point for those wishing to see Dante's ideas in the perspective of medieval political theory is Antony Black's *Politi-cal Thought in Europe 1250–1450*, Cambridge 1992, which contains a helpful bibliography. Other studies of great interest include E. H. Kantorowicz, *The King's Two Bodies. A Study in Medieval Political Theology* (ch. viii: 'Man-centred Kingship: Dante'), New Jersey 1981, pp. 451–95; D. Maffei, *La donazione di Costantino nei giuristi medievali*, Milano 1964; N. Rubinstein, 'The Beginnings of Political Thought in Florence', in *Journal of the Warburg and Courtauld Insti-tutes* 5, 1942, pp. 198–227; J. A. Watt, 'The Theory of Papal Mon-archy in the Thirteenth Century. The Contribution of the Canon-ists', in *Traditio* 20, 1964, pp. 179–317 (published as a book with the same title, London 1965).

Useful studies relating to the historical background of Dante's treatise are: T. S. R. Boase, *Boniface VIII*, London 1933; W. M. Bowsky, *Henry VII in Italy. The Conflict of Empire and City-State, 1310–1313*, Lincoln 1960; P. Contamine, *War in the Middle Ages* (translated by M. Jones), Oxford 1984; J. Larner, *Italy in the Age of Dante and Petrarch 1216–1380*, London and New York 1980; D. Waley, *The Italian City-Republics*, London 1969; and D. Waley, *The Papal State in the Thirteenth Century*, London 1961. A good general overview of the whole period is to be found in the relevant chapters of M. Keen, *The Pelican History of Medieval Europe*, Aylesbury 1969; of the history of Florence in Dante's time in F. Schevill, *History of Florence*, New York 1961; and of the state of historical research in relation to the period in N. Rubinstein, 'Studies on the Political History of the Age of Dante', in *Atti del Congresso Internazionale di Studi Danteschi*, Firenze 1965, pp. 225–47.

Monarchy

Book One

i

For all men whom the Higher Nature[1] has endowed with a love of
truth, this above all seems to be a matter of concern, that just as
they have been enriched by the efforts of their forebears, so they
too may work for future generations, in order that posterity may
be enriched by their efforts. For the man who is steeped in the 2
teachings which form our common heritage, yet has no interest in
contributing something to the community, is failing in his duty: let
him be in no doubt of that; for he is not 'a tree planted by the
rivers of water, that bringeth forth his fruit in due season',[2] but
rather a destructive whirlpool which forever swallows things down
and never gives back what it has swallowed. Thinking often about 3
these things, lest some day I be accused of burying my talent,[3] I
wish not just to put forth buds but to bear fruit for the benefit of
all, and to reveal truths that have not been attempted by others.[4]
For what fruit would a man bear who proved once again a theorem 4
of Euclid's? or who sought to show once again the nature of happi-

---

[1] i.e. God. The phrase is best glossed by *Mon.* II, ii, 2: 'nature in the mind of the
first mover, who is God'. Man's love of truth is the mark of his divine origin,
for it is God who has 'stamped' or 'imprinted' [*impressit*] him with the desire for
knowledge (see Introduction p. xv–xvi). The wax-and-seal metaphor for creation
implicit in the verb will become explicit at II, ii, 8 (see n. 8).

[2] Psalms 1, 3.

[3] The parable of the buried talent is in Matthew 25, 14–30.

[4] Dante's originality lies not in his choice of subject, much debated in the thirteenth
and early fourteenth century, but in his attempting to ground the discussion on
philosophical first principles and in the conclusions to which this leads.

ness, which has already been shown by Aristotle? or who took up the defence of old age which has already been defended by Cicero? None at all; indeed the tiresome pointlessness of the exercise would arouse distaste.

5 Now since among other truths which are hidden and useful, a knowledge of temporal monarchy is both extremely useful and most inaccessible, and since no one has attempted to elucidate it (on account of its not leading directly to material gain), I propose to draw it forth from where it lies hidden, so that my wakeful nights may be of benefit to the world, and so that I may be the first to
6 win for my own glory the honour of so great a prize.[5] It is indeed an arduous task, and one beyond my strength, that I embark on, trusting not so much in my own powers as in the light of that Giver who 'giveth to all men liberally, and upbraideth not'.[6]

ii

Firstly therefore we must see what is meant by 'temporal mon-
2 archy', in broad terms and as it is generally understood. Temporal monarchy, then, which men call 'empire', is a single sovereign authority set over all others in time, that is to say over all authorities which operate in those things and over those things which are meas-
3 ured by time.[1] Now there are three main points of inquiry which have given rise to perplexity on this subject: first, is it necessary to the well-being of the world? second, did the Roman people take on the office of the monarch by right? and third, does the monarch's authority derive directly from God or from someone else (his minister or vicar)?

4 Now since every truth which is not itself a first principle must be demonstrated with reference to the truth of some first principle, it is necessary in any inquiry to know the first principle to which

---

[5] Cf. 1 Corinthians 9, 24.

[6] James 1, 5.

[1] The definition has two key elements: temporal monarchy is one and indivisible [*unicus*]; and it is set over all other forms of temporal (i.e. secular) authority [*super omnes* (sc. *principatus*) *in tempore*], secular authority being distinguished from spiritual authority precisely by its relationship to 'things measured by time' as distinct from the eternal things of the spirit which are outside time. Cf. III, x. 10; 'empire is a jurisdiction which embraces within its scope every other temporal jurisdiction'.

we refer back in the course of strict deductive argument in order to ascertain the truth of all the propositions which are advanced later. And since this present treatise is a kind of inquiry, we must at the outset investigate the principle whose truth provides a firm foundation for later propositions. For it must be noted that there 5 are certain things (such as mathematics, the sciences and divinity[2]) which are outside human control, and about which we can only theorize, but which we cannot affect by our actions; and then there are certain things which are within our control, where we can not only theorize but also act, and in these action is not for the sake of theory, but theorizing is for the sake of taking action, since in these the objective is to take action. Now since our present subject is 6 political, indeed is the source and starting-point of just forms of government, and everything in the political sphere comes under human control, it is clear that the present subject is not directed primarily towards theoretical understanding but towards action. Again, since in actions it is the final objective[3] which sets in motion 7 and causes everything – for that is what first moves a person who acts – it follows that the whole basis of the means for attaining an end is derived from the end itself. For there will be one way of cutting wood to build a house, and another to build a ship. There- 8 fore whatever constitutes the purpose of the whole of human society (if there is such a purpose) will be here the first principle, in terms of which all subsequent propositions to be proved will be demonstrated with sufficient rigour; for it would be foolish to suppose that there is one purpose for this society and another for that, and not a common purpose for all of them.

iii

We must therefore now see what is the purpose of human society as a whole; when we have seen this, more than half our work will

[2] The distinction between the theoretical and practical sciences is Aristotelian, as are the three areas of theoretical enquiry here mentioned (for Dante as for Aristotle *physica* [the natural sciences] embraced all aspects of the study of the natural world, including biology, astronomy, meteorology, chemistry and physics); see J. Barnes, *Aristotle*, Oxford 1982, ch. 6: 'The structure of the sciences', pp. 23–7 and ch. 18: 'Practical philosophy', pp. 77–83.
[3] Final objective, goal, purpose, end [*ultimus finis*] is one of four kinds of cause distinguished by Aristotle, the others being material, formal and efficient. Brief

2 be done, as Aristotle says in the *Ethics*.[1] And to throw light on the matter we are inquiring into, it should be borne in mind that, just as there is a particular purpose for which nature produces the thumb, and a different one for which she produces the whole hand, and again a purpose different from both of these for which she produces the arm, and a purpose different from all of these for which she produces the whole person; in the same way there is one purpose for which the individual person is designed, another for the household, another for the small community, yet another for the city, and another for the kingdom; and finally the best purpose of all is the one for which God Everlasting with his art, which is nature, brings into being the whole of mankind. And it is this purpose we are seeking here as the guiding principle in our inquiry.

3 Consequently the first point to bear in mind is that God and nature do nothing in vain;[2] on the contrary whatever they bring into being is designed for a purpose. For in the intention of its creator *qua* creator the essential nature of any created being is not an ultimate end in itself; the end is rather the activity which is proper to that nature; and so it is that the activity does not exist for the sake of the essential nature, but the essential nature for the sake of that

4 activity. There is therefore some activity specific to humanity as a whole, for which the whole human race in all its vast number of individual human beings is designed; and no single person, or household, or small community, or city, or individual kingdom can fully achieve it. Now what this activity is will become clear when once we clarify what is the highest potentiality of the whole of

5 mankind. I say therefore that no faculty shared by many different species is the highest potentiality of any one of them; because, since it is precisely that highest potentiality which is the defining characteristic of the species, it would follow that one and the same essen-

6 tial nature was specific to several species; and this is impossible. So the highest faculty in a human being is not simply to exist, because the elements too share in the simple fact of existence; nor is it to

definitions of all four are to be found in Peter of Spain, *Tractatus called afterwards Summule Logicales* (henceforth *Summule*), ed. L. M. De Rijk, Assen 1972, pp. 67–69; and see P. Boyde, *Dante Philomythes and Philosopher. Man in the Cosmos*, Cambridge 1981, ch. 1: 'Wonder and knowledge', esp. pp. 51–4.

[1] *Ethics* 1, 7 1098b 6–7.

[2] This fundamental Aristotelian principle is the basis of the argument which follows in this chapter. On God and nature see also *Mon.* II, ii, 2–3.

exist in compound form, for that is found in minerals; nor is it to
exist as a living thing, for plants too share in that; nor is it to exist
as a creature with sense perception, for that is also shared by the
lower animals; but it is to exist as a creature who apprehends by
means of the potential intellect:[3] this mode of existence belongs to
no creature (whether higher or lower) other than human beings.
For while there are indeed other beings[4] who like us are endowed 7
with intellect, nonetheless their intellect is not 'potential' in the way
that man's is, since such beings exist only as intelligences and
nothing else, and their very being is simply the act of understanding
that their own nature exists; and they are engaged in this ceaselessly,
otherwise they would not be eternal. It is thus clear that the highest
potentiality of mankind is his intellectual potentiality or faculty.
And since that potentiality cannot be fully actualized all at once in 8
any one individual or in any one of the particular social groupings
enumerated above, there must needs be a vast number of individual
people in the human race, through whom the whole of this potentiality can be actualized; just as there must be a great variety of
things which can be generated so that the whole potentiality of
prime matter can continuously be actualized; otherwise one would
be postulating a potentiality existing separately from actualization,
which is impossible.[5] And Averroes is in agreement with this opi- 9
nion in his commentary on the *De anima*.[6] Now the intellectual
potentiality of which I am speaking is not only concerned with universal ideas or classes, but also (by extension as it were) with par-
ticulars; and so it is often said that the theoretical intellect by exten-

---

[3] Man's uniqueness resides in the duality of mind and body; because of this duality
his intellect (unlike that of angels) exists as a potentiality and not as something
which is always fully activated or operational, hence it is described as 'potential'
or 'possible'. Dante's view of humanity's place in the scale of creation is that of
an educated man of his time; see Boyde, *Dante Philomythes*, ch. 5: 'The natural
world and the Scale of Being', esp. pp. 123–31; on the activity characteristic of
a given nature [*propria operatio*] see Boyde, *Perception and Passion*, pp. 37–40.
[4] i.e. the celestial intelligences or angels, who are pure disembodied intellect. See
Boyde, *Dante Philomythes*, ch. 7: 'The angels', esp. pp. 186–98.
[5] On potentiality and actuality in the created world, and on becoming and being,
see Boyde, *Dante Philomythes*, pp. 60–2; and Barnes, pp. 46–51.
[6] Averroes, *De anima* III. Averroes (1126–98) is the great Moslem commentator on
Aristotle with whose view on the 'possible' intellect Dante elsewhere took issue;
see C. Vasoli, *Averroè*, in *ED* I, pp. 473–81, and *intelletto possibile*, in *ED* III, pp.
469–72; *Dict.*, pp. 75–6; Boyde, *Dante Philomythes*, pp. 276–8: 'The intellect and
the error of Averroes'.

10 sion becomes practical,[7] its goal then being *doing* and *making*.[8] I am referring to actions, which are regulated by political judgment, and to products, which are shaped by practical skill; all of these are subordinate to thinking as the best activity for which the Primal Goodness brought mankind into existence. This sheds light on that statement in the *Politics* that 'men of vigorous intellect naturally rule over others'.[9]

iv

Now it has been sufficiently explained that the activity proper to mankind considered as a whole is constantly to actualize the full intellectual potential of humanity, primarily through thought and secondarily through action (as a function and extension of thought).

2 And since what holds true for the part is true for the whole, and an individual human being 'grows perfect in judgment and wisdom when he sits at rest',[1] it is apparent that mankind most freely and readily attends to this activity – an activity which is almost divine, as we read in the psalm: 'Thou hast made him a little lower than the angels'[2] – in the calm or tranquillity of peace. Hence it is clear that universal peace is the best of those things which are ordained

3 for our human happiness. That is why the message which rang out from on high to the shepherds was not wealth, nor pleasures, nor honours, not long life, nor health, nor strength, nor beauty, but peace; for the heavenly host said: 'Glory to God on high, and on

---

[7] On the relationship between theoretical and practical intellect, see *Mon.* I, xiv, 7; and see Boyde, *Perception and Passion*, esp. pp. 177–85.

[8] 'Doing' and 'making' are the two modes of operation of the practical intellect (see Barnes, p. 27); these activities are controlled and directed respectively by wisdom in its two practical manifestations as judgment [*prudentia politica*] (see Antony Black, *Political Thought in Europe 1250–1450*, Cambridge 1992, p. 158) and skill or expertise [*ars*].

[9] Aristotle nowhere says exactly this, but cf. *Politics* I, 2 1252a 31. Opinion is divided on whether Dante had a first-hand knowledge of the *Politics*, see A. H. Gilbert, 'Had Dante read the *Politics* of Aristotle?' in *PMLA*, XLIII 1928, pp. 602–13; L. Minio-Paluello, 'Dante's Reading of Aristotle', in *The World of Dante. Essays on Dante and his Times*, edited by C. Grayson, Oxford 1980, pp. 61–80; and E. Berti, *Politica*, in *ED* IV, pp. 585–7.

[1] The connection between the contemplative life and wisdom is a medieval commonplace (cf. Ecclesiasticus 38, 25; Aristotle, *Physics* 7, 3, 247b 10–11).

[2] Psalms 8, 6 (AV 8, 5).

earth peace to men of good will.'[3] And that is why the Saviour of 4
men used the greeting 'Peace be with you',[4] for it was fitting that
the supreme Saviour should utter the supreme salutation; and his
disciples and Paul chose to preserve this custom in their own greet-
ings, as everybody can verify. From the arguments developed so 5
far, it is clear what is the better, indeed the best, way of enabling
mankind to engage in the activity proper to humanity; and consequently we see the most direct means of achieving the goal to which
all our human actions are directed as to their final end. That means
is universal peace, which is to be taken as the first principle for the
arguments which follow. As we said, it was necessary to have such 6
a principle to serve as an agreed point of reference to which anything which had to be proved might be referred back, as to a self-
evident truth.

V

Returning then to the point made at the beginning,[1] there are three
main points of inquiry concerning temporal monarchy (or 'empire'
as it is more commonly called) which have given rise to and continue to give rise to perplexity; and as we have already said, it is
our intention to investigate these questions in the order in which
we set them out and taking the principle we have just established
as our starting-point. So the first question is this: is temporal mon- 2
archy necessary for the well-being of the world? That it *is* necessary
can be shown with powerful and persuasive arguments, and neither
reason nor authority provides any strong counter-argument. The
first of these arguments may be taken from the authority of Aristotle
in his *Politics*.[2] Now this revered authority states in that work that 3
when a number of things are ordered to a single end, one of them
must guide or direct, and the others be guided or directed; and it
is not only the author's illustrious name which requires us to believe

---

[3] Luke 2, 14.
[4] Luke 24, 36; John 20, 21; cf. also Matthew 10, 12.
[1] Having established his fundamental principles (what mankind's purpose is and
the means of achieving that purpose) Dante now returns to the three questions
formulated in I, ii.
[2] *Politics* I, 5.

4 this, but inductive reasoning as well. For if we consider a single person, we shall see that what happens in the individual is this: while all the faculties are directed towards happiness, it is the intellectual faculty which guides and directs all the others; otherwise

5 happiness is unattainable. If we consider a household, whose purpose is to prepare its members to live the good life, there must be one person who guides and directs, who is called the 'pater familias' or his representative, in line with Aristotle's observation that 'Every household is governed by the eldest';[3] and his role, as Homer says, is to guide everyone and impose rules on the others. Hence the

6 proverbial curse: 'May you have an equal in your house.' If we consider a small community, whose purpose is neighbourly support in relation both to people and to goods, there must be one person who guides the others, either appointed by someone from outside or emerging as leader from among their number with the agreement of the others ; otherwise not only will they fail to achieve that neighbourly collaboration, but sometimes, if a number of people contest

7 the leadership, the whole community is destroyed. If we consider a city, whose purpose is to be self-sufficient in living the good life,[4] there must be one ruling body, and this is so not only in just government, but in perverted forms of government as well; if this should not be the case, not only is the purpose of social life

8 thwarted, but the city itself ceases to be what it was. Lastly, if we consider an individual kingdom – and the purpose of a kingdom is the same as that of a city, but with greater confidence that peace can be maintained – there must be one king who rules and governs; otherwise not only do those who live in the kingdom not achieve that purpose, but the kingdom itself falls to ruin, in accordance with those words of the infallible Truth: 'Every kingdom divided

---

[3] This line from the *Odyssey* (IX, 114) is quoted in *Politics* 1, 2 1252b 20. Dante had no direct knowledge of Homer (see P. Toynbee, *Dante Studies and Researches*, London 1902, pp. 204–15).

[4] This definition is Aristotelian, see *Politics* 3, 9 1280b 29–34. To live the 'good life' is to live as a human being in the fullest sense, to live the life of a rational creature who applies reason to making discriminations of right and wrong, good and evil; a community achieves the 'good life' when it provides the conditions which enable its citizens to fulfil themselves in this way; see Barnes, pp. 77–83. Dante's review of social groupings of increasing size, from family to state, echoes Aristotle, *Politics* 1, 2, although for Aristotle the city-state was the largest such entity; Dante adds 'kingdom' to the list.

against itself shall be laid waste.'[5] If this holds true in these cases 9
and in individuals who are ordered to one particular goal, then the
proposition advanced above is true;[6] now it is agreed that the whole
of mankind is ordered to one goal, as has already been demonstrated:[7] there must therefore be one person who directs and rules
mankind, and he is properly called 'Monarch' or 'Emperor'. And 10
thus it is apparent that the well-being of the world requires that
there be a monarchy or empire.

vi

And as a part stands in relation to the whole, so the order in a part
stands to the order in the whole. A part stands in relation to the
whole as to its end and perfection: therefore the order in a part
stands to the order in the whole as to its end and perfection. From
this it can be deduced that the goodness of the order in a part does
not exceed the goodness of the order in the whole, but rather the
reverse. Now since there are two kinds of order observable in 2
things, i.e. the order which relates part to part, and the order which
relates the parts to some other entity which is not a part (thus the
component parts of an army are interrelated one to another, and
they are related to their commander[1]), the order of the parts in
relation to that single entity is better, for it constitutes the end or
purpose of their interrelationship; their interrelationship exists for
the sake of their relationship to the single entity, and not vice versa.
So if this second kind of order is discernible in the constituent parts 3
which make up the human race, then with all the more reason must
it be observable (by the force of our earlier syllogism[2]) in the human
race considered as a whole or totality, given that it is a better order

---

[5] Matthew 12, 25; Luke 11, 17.
[6] The proposition advanced in par. 3 is supported by the evidence surveyed in
pars. 4–8; it thus has the backing not only of Aristotle's authority but also of
inductive reasoning working on the observable facts.
[7] In chapter iii.
[1] The example of the army and its commander was a common one. Dante elsewhere
used the example of the crew of a ship to make the same point about parts in
relation to a whole. Both examples ultimately derive from Aristotle, *Metaphysics*
12, 10 and *Politics* 3, 4.
[2] The syllogism is that characteristic form of argument in Aristotelian logic which
allows valid deductive inference, see I, xi, n. 2. The syllogism here referred to is
the one enunciated in the first paragraph of this chapter.

or kind of order; but it *is* found in all the parts which make up the human race, as is quite clear from what was said in the previous
4 chapter:[3] therefore it must be observable in the totality.[4] And thus all the parts we have enumerated which are lower than kingdoms, and those kingdoms themselves, must be ordered to one ruler or one rule, that is to a monarch or monarchy.

vii

Furthermore, the human race constitutes a whole in relation to its constituent parts, and is itself a part in relation to a whole. It is a whole in relation to individual kingdoms and peoples, as has been shown above; and it is a part in relation to the whole universe. So
2 much is self-evident. And just as the lesser parts which make up the human race are well adapted to it, so it too can be described as being well adapted to its whole; for its parts are well adapted to it in relation to a single principle, as can easily be deduced from what was said earlier: and so absolutely speaking it too is well adapted to the universe (or to its ruler, who is God and Monarch)
3 in relation to a single principle, i.e. one ruler. And thus it follows that monarchy is necessary to the well-being of the world.

viii

And every thing is in a good (indeed, ideal) state which is in harmony with the intention of the first mover, who is God; and this is self-evident, except to those who deny that divine goodness attains
2 the summit of perfection. It is God's intention that every created thing should show forth His likeness in so far as its own nature can receive it. For this reason it is said: 'Let us make man in our image, after our likeness';[1] for although 'in our image' cannot be said of things lower than man, 'after our likeness' can be said of anything,[2]

---

[3] i.e. in pars. 4–8 of ch. v.

[4] The shaping principle reflected in the ordering or structuring of reality and the interrelatedness of part to part and of part to whole is one aspect of the universe's 'likeness' to God; cf. *Mon.* II, vi, 4 and I, viii, 2.

[1] Genesis I, 26. Boyde, *Dante Philomythes*, pp. 224–9, gives an account of the universe as bearing God's 'likeness' or 'imprint'.

[2] The distinction turns on man's rationality, which includes memory, intelligence and will, attributes not shared by the lower orders of creation, which nonetheless reflect divine goodness in their order or structure.

since the whole universe is simply an imprint of divine goodness.
So mankind is in a good (indeed, ideal) state when, to the extent
that its nature allows, it resembles God. But mankind most closely 3
resembles God when it is most a unity, since the true measure of
unity is in him alone; and for this reason it is written: 'Hear, o
Israel, the Lord thy God is one.'[3] But mankind is most a unity 4
when it is drawn together to form a single entity, and this can only
come about when it is ruled as one whole by one ruler, as is self-
evident. Therefore mankind is most like God when it is ruled by 5
one ruler, and consequently is most in harmony with God's intention; and this is what it means to be in a good (indeed, ideal) state,
as we established at the beginning of this chapter.

ix

Again, every son is in a good (indeed, ideal) state when he follows
in the footsteps of a perfect father, insofar as his own nature allows.
Mankind is the son of heaven, which is quite perfect in all its
workings; for man and the sun generate man, as we read in the
second book of the *Physics*.[1] Therefore mankind is in its ideal state
when it follows the footsteps of heaven, insofar as its nature allows.
And since the whole sphere of heaven is guided by a single move- 2
ment (i.e. that of the Primum Mobile), and by a single source of
motion (who is God), in all its own parts, movements and causes of
movement, as human understanding perceives quite clearly through
philosophical reasoning, then if our argument is sound,[2] mankind
is in its ideal state when it is guided by a single ruler (as by a single
source of motion) and in accordance with a single law (as by a
single movement) in its own causes of movement and in its own
movements.[3] Hence it is clear that monarchy (or that undivided 3

---

[3] Deuteronomy 6, 4 and Mark 12, 29.
[1] *Physics* 2, 2. Dante's views on human generation are those of his age and derive
from Aristotle, as he here indicates. (The woman's contribution to fertility, in
the form of the ovum, is a relatively recent discovery.) For a fuller account of
Dante's understanding of the process of human conception, including the Christian notion of the soul infused into the body directly by God at a certain stage
in foetal development, see Boyde, *Dante Philomythes*, ch. 11: 'The makings of a
man', esp. pp. 249–50, 271–9.
[2] Literally, if our syllogism is valid; see I, xi, n. 2.
[3] Dante sets up an exact analogy from macrocosm to microcosm along these lines:
as God and the Primum Mobile are to the workings of the universe (the 'whole

rule which is called 'empire') is necessary to the well-being of the world. Boethius expressed this view when he sighed:

> O happy race of men,
> if only the love by which the heavens are ruled
> might rule your minds.[4]

X

Now wherever there can be conflict there must be judgment to resolve it, otherwise there would be an imperfection without its proper corrective; and this is impossible, since God and nature

2 never fail in their provision of what is necessary.[1] There is always the possibility of conflict between two rulers where one is not subject to the other's control; such conflict may come about either through their own fault or the fault of their subjects (the point is

3 self-evident); therefore there must be judgment between them. And since neither can judge the other (since neither is under the other's control, and an equal has no power over an equal) there must be a third party of wider jurisdiction who rules over both of them by

4 right. And this person will either be the monarch or not. If he is, then our point is proved; if he is not, he in his turn will have an equal who is outside the sphere of *his* jurisdiction, and then it will

5 once again be necessary to have recourse to a third party. And so either this procedure will continue *ad infinitum*, which is not possible, or else we must come to a first and supreme judge, whose judgment resolves all disputes either directly or indirectly;[2] and this man will be the monarch or emperor. Thus monarchy is necessary

6 to the world. And Aristotle saw the force of this argument when

sphere of heaven' [*celum totum*] is the whole of the created world contained within the sphere of the Primum Mobile according to Ptolemaic astronomy), so the monarch and the law should be to the workings of human society, being respectively the source of action and the mechanism by which action is regulated. A lucid and informative account of Dante's cosmology which links it to notions of cause and purpose in ways which throw light on this passage is to be found in Boyde, *Dante Philomythes*, ch. 6: 'Concerning the heavens', esp. pp. 132–43; see also C. S. Lewis, *The Discarded Image*, Cambridge 1964, ch. 5: 'The heavens', pp. 92–121.

[4] *De consolatione philosophiae* II, metr. 8.

[1] A philosophical commonplace which is a corollary to the earlier 'God and nature do nothing in vain'.

[2] i.e. in practical terms either as a court of first appeal or on appeal from a lower court.

he said: 'Things do not wish to be badly ordered; a plurality of reigns is bad; therefore let there be one ruler.'[3]

xi

Furthermore, the world is ordered in the best possible way when justice is at its strongest in it. Thus Virgil, wishing to praise the age which seemed to be emerging in his day, sang in his *Eclogues*:

> Now the Virgin returns, the reign of Saturn returns.[1]

For 'the virgin' was their name for justice, whom they also called 'Astrea'; the 'reign of Saturn' was their name for the best of times, which they also called 'golden'. Justice is at its strongest only under 2 a monarch; therefore for the best ordering of the world there must be a monarchy or empire. To clarify the minor premiss,[2] it must be 3 understood that justice, considered in itself and in its own nature, is a kind of rectitude or rule[3] which spurns deviation from the straight

---

[3] *Metaphysics* 12, 10. Aristotle here cites Homer on Agamemnon (Iliad II, 204), although he is referring not to a worldly prince but to the unmoved mover.

[1] *Eclogue* IV, 6.

[2] The syllogism, as noted, is that form of argument which allows valid deductive inference in Aristotelian logic; it consists always of three statements: major premiss, minor premiss, conclusion. If the syllogism is valid, then once the major and minor premisses have been established, the conclusion follows with logical inevitability. The link between the premisses is established by the 'middle' term (cf. *Mon.* III, vii, 3) which they have in common; the minor premiss itself is the link between major premiss and conclusion. A syllogism will be invalid if certain logical errors are made (and Dante will expose the faulty reasoning in a series of invalid syllogisms used by his opponents in *Mon.* III, iv, 21–22; v, 3; vii, 3); it will be valid but untrue if either major or minor premiss is untrue (see *Mon.* III, v, 4–5). Dante characteristically argues by enunciating a syllogism which is logically valid (i.e. the conclusion follows from the premisses), then proving the major and minor premisses to establish that its content is true. There are three types (or figures) of syllogism, classified according to the position of the 'middle' term in the premisses (subject in one and predicate in the other; predicate in both; subject in both). Useful brief accounts of syllogistic argument are to be found in J. L. Ackrill, *Aristotle the Philosopher*, Oxford 1981, ch. 6: 'Logic', pp. 79–93; and R. Smith, 'Logic', in *The Cambridge Companion to Aristotle*, ed. J. Barnes, Cambridge 1995, pp. 27–65.

[3] Although Aristotle devotes a large section of the *Ethics* to justice, and uses geometrical notions of proportion to clarify it (cf. *Mon.* II, v, 1 on 'right' [*ius*]), he nowhere (I think) formulates a definition in these terms of 'straightness' (or 'rectilinearity') and 'deviation from the straight line'. It has been argued that this is not a definition but a simile used to underline the absolute quality of justice considered in the abstract.

path to either side; and thus it does not admit of a more and a less – just like whiteness considered in the abstract.[4]

4   There are forms of this kind, in fact, which are to be found in composites, but which in themselves consist of a simple and unchangeable essence, as the Master of the Six Principles[5] rightly says. Such qualities are present to a greater or lesser degree depending on the subjects in which they are given concrete form, according as these subjects contain more or less of their opposites.

5   Therefore justice is at its strongest where there is least of what is opposed to justice both in the disposition and in the actions of an agent; and then truly it can be said of her, as Aristotle says, 'neither Hesperus nor Lucifer is so wondrous'. For she is then like Phoebe gazing across the heavens at her brother from the rosy flush of the clear morning sky, from a point on the horizon diametrically

6   opposite.[6] As far as disposition is concerned, justice is sometimes impeded in the will; for where the will is not entirely free of all greed, even if justice is present, nonetheless it is not entirely present in the splendour of its purity; for the subject[7] has something, however slight, which is in some way resistant to it; and this is why those who try to stir up a judge's emotions are rightly rebuffed.[8]

---

[4] Concepts such as 'justice' and 'whiteness', considered in themselves (i.e. in the abstract), consist of a simple and unvarying essence; in practice such abstractions are observable in our world only in concrete 'subjects' (the individual who enacts justice, the thing which is white) and the nature of the subject in any given instance will determine how 'pure' or 'impure' they are, i.e. to what degree they are 'mixed' with or 'contaminated' by what is opposed to them. What is opposed to justice, Dante will now go on to explain, takes two forms: it may be in the disposition of the subject, i.e. in his will, which can be incapacitated by greed, which is self-serving (egotistical) and thus in conflict with justice itself which is altruistic [*ad alterum*], concerned with the welfare of others and the common good; or it may be in action, if the subject lacks the power to act in relation to what he perceives to be just and wishes to do.

[5] The author of a Commentary on Aristotle's *Categories*, often wrongly identified with Gilbertus Porretanus or Gilbert de la Porrée, Bishop of Poitiers; see L. Minio Paluello, 'Magister Sex Principiorum', in *Studi medievali*, s. 3, VI (1965), pp. 123–51; and *ED* III, p. 767.

[6] The quotation, from a lost tragedy of Euripides, is cited by Aristotle in *Ethics* 5, 1 1129b 28–9. Hesperus = the evening star, Lucifer = the morning star (i.e. the planet Venus in its two aspects); Phoebe = Diana, the moon; her brother = the sun; i.e. where justice shines in its full splendour it outshines even the brightest star or planet and is comparable to the full moon shining in the clear dawn sky.

[7] i.e. the person who is enacting justice.

[8] Such people obstruct justice by interfering with the judge's ability to function as he ought, which requires precisely that he be 'dispassionate', free of emotions [*passiones*].

As far as actions are concerned, justice is sometimes impeded with 7
regard to power; for since justice is a virtue that operates in relation
to other people,[9] if someone does not have the power to give to
each person what is his, how will he act in accordance with justice?
From this it is clear that the more powerful a just man is, the more
effectively will justice be brought about by his actions.

Building on this exposition we can argue as follows: justice is at 8
its strongest in the world when it resides in a subject who has in
the highest degree possible the will and the power to act; only the
monarch is such a subject; therefore justice is at its strongest in the
world when it is located in the monarch alone. This prosyllogism[10] 9
is of the second figure with intrinsic negation, and it takes this form:
all B is A; only C is A; therefore only C is B. That is: all B is A;
nothing except C is A; therefore nothing except C is B. And the 10
first proposition[11] is established by the preceding exposition; the
second is shown as follows, firstly in relation to volition, and then
in relation to power. To clarify the first of these[12] it must be noted 11
that the thing most contrary to justice is greed, as Aristotle states
in the fifth book of the *Ethics*.[13] When greed is entirely eliminated,
nothing remains which is opposed to justice; hence Aristotle's opinion[14] that those things which can be resolved by law should in no

---

[9] i.e. it is not self-serving or egotistical, but directed towards one's fellow-man and
the common good, cf. *Ethics* 5, 1 1129b 26–1130a 13.

[10] A prosyllogism is a preparatory or subsidiary syllogism in the context of the argument developed in the chapter as a whole; here the prosyllogism is introduced to
prove the minor premiss of the main syllogism. This prosyllogism is of type 2
(see n. 2 above: A is the predicate in both premisses), with an excluding or limiting
(hence 'negative') minor premiss ('only the monarch', 'no one but the monarch'
has the qualities referred to); this negative element is 'intrinsic', i.e. implicit in
the definition of the word 'monarch'. (The reformulation of the prosyllogism with
'nothing except' in the place of 'only' serves to underline the negative element,
which is a characteristic of second figure syllogisms.) The main syllogism is the
one enunciated at the beginning of the chapter, whose major premiss is self-
evidently true (and is incidentally illustrated by the Virgilian quotation), but
whose minor premiss is by no means self-evident and must therefore be demonstrated, starting with a clarification of the meaning of the term 'justice', pars. 3–7.

[11] The 'first proposition' is the major premiss of the prosyllogism (demonstrated in
pars. 5–7); the second is the minor premiss of the prosyllogism, which Dante now
proceeds to prove.

[12] i.e. how justice relates to volition.

[13] Dante's view of greed [*cupiditas*] draws on both Aristotle, *Ethics* 5, 1 1129a 32–
b 10 and 2 1130a 16–32, and the Bible, 1 Timothy 6, 10 [*radix enim omnium
malorum est cupiditas*]; cf. *Mon.* I, xiii, 7: 'it is greed alone which perverts judgment
and obstructs justice'.

[14] *Rhetoric* 1, 1; the idea had become a commonplace.

way be left to the judge's discretion. And it is fear of greed which makes this necessary, for greed easily leads men's minds astray. But where there is nothing which can be coveted, it is impossible for greed to exist, for emotions cannot exist where their objects have

12 been destroyed. But there is nothing the monarch *could* covet, for his jurisdiction is bounded only by the ocean;[15] whereas this is not the case with other rulers, whose sovereignty extends only as far as the neighbouring kingdom, as is the case, for instance, with the kings of Castille and of Aragon.[16] From this it follows that of all

13 men the monarch can be the purest embodiment of justice. Moreover, just as greed, however slight, dulls the habit of justice in some way, so charity or rightly ordered love[17] makes it sharper and brighter. So the man in whom rightly ordered love can be strongest is the one in whom justice can have its principal abode; the monarch is such a man; therefore justice is or can be at its strongest when

14 he exists. That rightly ordered love does what has been stated can be deduced from this: greed, scorning the intrinsic nature of man, seeks other things; whereas love, scorning all other things, seeks God and man, and hence the true good of man. Since among the other goods available to man living in peace is supremely important (as we saw earlier), and justice principally and most effectively brings this about, love most of all will strengthen justice, and the

15 stronger love is the more it will do so. And that the monarch more than all other men should feel rightly ordered love can be shown as follows: the closer any loved object is to the lover the more it is loved; but men are closer to the monarch than to other princes; therefore they are more loved by him, or ought to be. The first premiss is clear if we take into consideration the nature of agents and patients;[18] the second becomes clear if we bear in mind this

[15] i.e. his jurisdiction covers the whole of the inhabited land mass; no territory or person lies outside it. This appears to be a deliberate echo of *Aen.* I, 286–7: *nascetur pulchra Troianus origine Caesar, / imperium Oceano, famam qui terminet astris* ('From this noble line shall be born the Trojan Caesar, who shall limit his empire with ocean, his glory with the stars').

[16] A contemporary example of the conflict which arises between finite kingdoms when there is no superior and all-embracing power to act as a judge and resolve conflict.

[17] Augustine in *De civitate Dei* 14, 7 points out that *amor* and *dilectio* (unlike *karitas*) are used with reference to both good and evil; Aquinas in *Summa theologiae*, Ia. 60, 1 makes the same point about *dilectio*. Hence Dante's need to specify 'rightly directed love' [*recta dilectio*].

[18] In this context agent = the lover and patient = the loved one.

fact, that men are close to other rulers only as parts, but they are close to the monarch as a totality.[19] Again, they are close to other rulers by virtue of the monarch, and not vice versa; and thus concern for all men's welfare is primarily and directly the monarch's concern; other rulers share in it through the monarch, since their concern derives from that higher concern of his. Besides, the more universal a cause is, the more truly it is a cause, because the lower is not a cause except by virtue of the higher, as is clear from the *De causis*;[20] and the more truly a cause is a cause, the more it loves its own effect, since this love follows from the cause as such. Therefore since the monarch is the most universal cause among mortals that men should live the good life (for other rulers are a cause only by virtue of him, as we have seen), it follows that the good of mankind is dear to him above all else. Who doubts that the monarch is most strongly disposed to the working of justice, except those who do not understand the meaning of the word, since, if he is monarch, he cannot have enemies? The minor premiss of the main syllogism has been sufficiently proved and the conclusion is certain, namely that the best ordering of the world requires the existence of a monarchy.

xii

Now the human race is in its ideal state when it is completely free. This will be clear if we clarify the principle of freedom. Therefore it must be borne in mind that the first principle of our freedom is free will,[1] which many people talk about but few understand. For they go so far as to say that free will is free judgment in matters of volition. And what they say is true, but they are very far from understanding what the words mean, just like our logicians who daily enunciate certain propositions by way of example in their discussions on logic, such as 'a triangle has three angles equal to two

[19] The distinction made here is clarified by *Mon.* I, xiv, 4–7.
[20] The anonymous *Liber de causis* (often wrongly attributed to Aristotle, though not by Dante) was the prime source of neo-platonic ideas on scholasticism, see *ED* II, pp. 327–9; *Dict.*, p. 159.
[1] On Dante's understanding of human freedom of the will, see Boyde, *Perception and Passion*, ch. 10 'Aspects of human freedom', pp. 193–214.

3 right angles'.[2] And therefore I say that judgment is the link between perception and appetition: for first a thing is perceived, then it is judged to be good or evil, and finally the person who
4 judges pursues it or shuns it. Now if judgment controls desire completely and is in no way pre-empted by it, it is free; but if judgment is in any way at all pre-empted and thus controlled by desire, it cannot be free, because it does not act under its own power, but is dragged along in the power of something else.
5 And that is why the lower animals cannot have free will, because their judgments are always pre-empted by desire. And from this it is also clear that non-material beings,[3] whose wills are unchangeable, as well as human souls who leave this world of ours in a state of grace, do not lose free will on account of the fact that their wills are unchangeable; in fact they retain it in its most perfect and true form.
6 When this has been grasped, it can also be seen that this freedom (or this principle of all our freedom) is the greatest gift given by God to human nature – as I have already said in the Paradiso of the *Comedy* [4] – since by virtue of it we become happy here as men,
7 by virtue of it we become happy elsewhere as gods. If this is the case, who will not agree that the human race is at its best when it
8 is able to make fullest use of this principle? But living under a monarch it is supremely free. Thus it must be borne in mind that a thing is free which exists 'for its own sake and not for the sake of something else', as Aristotle states in the *Metaphysics*.[5] For a thing which exists for the sake of something else is necessarily conditioned by that other for whose sake it exists, as a route is necessar-
9 ily conditioned by its terminus. Mankind exists for its own sake and not for the sake of something else only when it is under the

---

[2] The implication is that such propositions are repeated mechanically, as in rote learning, with no real understanding. The example of the angles of a triangle is used repeatedly by Aristotle by way of illustration in the *Posterior Analytics* and the *Sophistical Refutations*.

[3] i.e. angels.

[4] Cf. *Paradiso* v, 19–24: Lo maggior don che Dio per sua larghezza / fesse creando ... / fu della volontà la libertate; / di che le creature intelligenti, / e tutte e sole, fuoro e son dotate ('The greatest gift that God in his bounty bestowed in the act of creation ... was freedom of the will, with which all intelligent beings, and they alone, were and are endowed.'). This cross-reference to the *Paradiso* is crucial for the dating of the *Monarchy* (see Introduction, p. xxxiii).

[5] *Metaphysics* I, 2 982b 25–6.

rule of a monarch, for only then are perverted forms of government (i.e. democracies, oligarchies and tyrannies[6]), which force mankind into slavery, set right – as is clear to anyone who examines them all; and only then do kings, aristocrats (known as the great and the good), and those zealous for the freedom of the people govern justly; for since the monarch loves men most, as we have already noted,[7] he wants all men to become good; and this cannot happen under perverted forms of government. Hence Aristotle in the *Politics*[8] says 10 that in bad government the good man is a bad citizen, whereas in good government the good man and the good citizen are one and the same thing. And these just forms of government aim at freedom, i.e. that men should exist for their own sake. For citizens do not 11 exist for the sake of consuls, nor the people for the sake of the king, but on the contrary consuls exist for the sake of the citizens and the king for the people; for just as a political community is not formed for the sake of the laws, but the laws are framed for the benefit of the political community, in the same way those whose lives are governed by the law are not there for the sake of the legislator, but rather he is there for their sake, as Aristotle says in those writings he left to us on this subject.[9] Thus it is apparent that, 12 although a consul or a king are masters over others with respect to means, with respect to ends they are the servants of others; and this is especially true of the monarch, who is to be considered without doubt the servant of all men. Thus it is already clear that the very same goal which requires the formulation of laws requires also that there be a monarch. Therefore mankind living under a mon- 13 arch is in its ideal state; from this it follows that monarchy is necessary for the well-being of the world.

---

[6] These are Aristotle's three forms of faulty or perverted government ('democracy' here meaning demagogy or rule of the mob), contrasted (in inverse order) with the corresponding forms of good government. Good governments are those which give their citizens freedom (see par. 10) and thus enable them to lead the good life. See *Politics* 3, 7.

[7] i.e. in the previous chapter (pars. 13–15).

[8] Again Aristotle does not say exactly this, but he considers the question in *Politics* 3, 4; Aquinas in his commentary on *Ethics* 5, 3 says precisely this.

[9] *Politics* 4, 1 1289a 13–15.

xiii

Besides, the person who is himself capable of being best disposed to rule is capable of disposing others best,[1] for in every action the primary aim of the agent, whether it act because its nature compels it to or as a matter of free choice, is to reproduce its own likeness.[2]

2 Hence every agent, precisely as agent, takes pleasure in its own action; for since everything which exists desires its own being, and in acting the agent's being is in some sense enhanced, of necessity pleasure ensues, since pleasure is always connected to something which is desired.

3 Therefore nothing acts unless it has the qualities which are to be communicated to the thing acted upon; hence Aristotle in the *Metaphysics* says: 'The movement from potentiality to actuality comes about by means of something which is already actual';[3] any attempt to do otherwise would be a vain attempt.

4 And thus we can refute the error of those who, expressing worthy sentiments and doing wrong, nonetheless believe they can influence the lives and behaviour of others, not realizing that Jacob's hands carried more weight than his words, even though his hands deceived and his words revealed the truth.[4] Hence Aristotle in the *Ethics* says: 'In matters where passions and actions are involved, words carry

5 less conviction than actions.'[5] Hence a voice from heaven asked the sinner David: 'Why do you tell of my righteousness?',[6] as if to say: 'You speak in vain, since your words are belied by what you are.' From which it can be deduced that a person who wishes to dispose

6 others for the best must himself be disposed for the best. But only the monarch can be best disposed for ruling. This can be explained

---

[1] It has been suggested that this opening statement, with its careful repetition of 'is capable of' [*potest*], may reflect Dante's awareness of the gap between his ideal monarch (as described in the previous chapters) and possible shortcomings in an actual incumbent. The abstract nature of Dante's monarch was as it happens savagely attacked by Guido Vernani, his earliest critic, who argued that only Christ could have the qualities Dante ascribes to him.

[2] On this point and its development in par. 2, see Boyde, *Dante Philomythes*, p. 257.

[3] *Metaphysics* 9, 8 1049b 24–26; cf. *Mon.* III, xiii, 6; see Boyde, *Dante Philomythes*, pp. 60–2, 255.

[4] Genesis 27, 1 f. Although Jacob's true identity was revealed by his voice, his hands (disguised with goatskin to make them feel hairy) seemed to be those of Esau, and were taken as the more convincing evidence of identity by Isaac.

[5] *Ethics* 10, 1.

[6] Psalms 49, 16 (AV 50, 16).

as follows: any thing is the more easily and perfectly disposed to acquire a particular disposition and to act in accordance with it, the less there is in it which is opposed to that disposition; thus those who have never studied philosophy acquire the habit of philosophical truth more easily and perfectly than those who have studied for a long time and become familiar with false notions. So that Galen rightly comments that such people take twice as long to acquire knowledge.[7] Therefore since the monarch can have no occasion for greed (or in any event of all men the very least occasion), as we saw earlier[8] (and this is *not* the case with other rulers), and since it is greed alone which perverts judgment and obstructs justice, it follows that he alone, or he more than anyone else, can be well disposed to rule, since of all men he can have judgment and justice in the highest degree. These are the two chief qualities needed by the legislator and the executor of the law, as that holy king bore witness when he asked God for those things needed by the king and the king's son: 'God', he said, 'give your judgment to the king and your justice to the king's son.'[9] What was affirmed in the minor premiss is therefore quite correct, i.e. that the monarch alone is the person who can be best disposed to rule: therefore the monarch alone can best dispose other people. It follows from this that monarchy is necessary to the well-being of the world.

xiv

And what can be brought about by a single agent is better done by a single agent than by more than one.[1] This can be explained as follows: let there be one agent (A) by which something can be brought about, and let there be several agents (A and B) by which it can equally be brought about; now if that same thing which can be brought about by means of A and B can be brought about by A alone, then B is introduced unnecessarily, because nothing is achieved by the introduction of B, since that same thing was already achieved by means of A alone. And since the introduction of any

---

[7] Galen, *De cognoscendis curandisque animi morbis*, 10.
[8] i.e. in ch. xi, pars. 11–12.
[9] Psalms 71, 1 (AV 72, 1). David asks God for wisdom for his son Solomon.
[1] The 'principle of the sufficient cause' is an application of the principle that God does not like *superfluum*, as is explained in this and the following paragraph.

such means is unnecessary and pointless, and everything which is pointless is displeasing to God and to nature, and everything which is displeasing to God and to nature is evil (as is self-evident), it follows that not only is it better that something should be brought about by a single agent, where that is possible, rather than by several, but that being brought about by a single agent is good, by

3 more than one is in absolute terms bad.[2] Moreover, a thing is said to be better the closer it is to the best; and the goal itself is the measure of what is best; but to be brought about by a single agent is closer[3] to the goal; therefore it is better. And that it is closer can be shown as follows: let the goal be C; let the achieving of that goal by a single agent be A, and by several agents be A and B; it is clear that to go from A through B to C is a longer route than to go from

4 A directly to C. But mankind can be ruled by one supreme ruler, who is the monarch. On this point it must of course be noted that when we say 'mankind can be ruled by one supreme ruler', this is not to be taken to mean that trivial decisions in every locality can be made directly by him – even though it can happen that local laws are sometimes defective and there may be a need for guidance in implementing them, as is clear from what Aristotle says in the fifth book of the *Ethics* when he commends the principle of equity.[4]

5 For nations, kingdoms and cities have characteristics of their own, which need to be governed by different laws; for law is a rule which

6 governs life. Thus the Scythians, who live beyond the seventh zone and are exposed to nights and days of very unequal length, and who endure an almost unbearable intensity of cold, need to have one set of laws, while the Garamantes require different laws, since they live in the equatorial zone and always have days and nights of equal length, and because of the excessive heat of the air cannot

7 bear to cover themselves with clothes.[5] It is rather to be understood

---

[2] To choose the less 'economic' or 'efficient' means is 'simply' or 'in absolute terms' bad.

[3] It is 'closer' in the sense of reaching the goal by a more direct (i.e. more economical) route, involving no *superfluum*.

[4] The principle of equity [*epyikia*] is recommended by Aristotle (*Ethics* 5, 10 1137a 31–1138a 2) when general laws need to be applied to particular cases not envisaged specifically in the legislation. It is discussed by Aquinas in *Summa Theologiae*, 2a 2ae, q. 120, art. 1 [*epicheia quae apud nos dicitur aequitas*], and in Lecture XVI of Book V *In Eth.*

[5] The Scythians and the Garamantes represent the extreme limits of the inhabitable land mass according to Dante's world view, occupying respectively the arctic region (specifically, north of the Black Sea and NE of the Caspian) and the equa-

in this sense, that mankind is to be ruled by him in those matters
which are common to all men and of relevance to all, and is to be
guided towards peace by a common law. This rule or law should
be received from him by individual rulers, just as the practical intellect, in order to proceed to action, receives the major premiss from
the theoretical intellect, and then derives the minor premiss appropriate to its own particular case, and then proceeds to the action in
question.[6] And it is not only possible for one person to do this, but 8
necessary for this to come from one person, to avoid any confusion
about universal principles. Moses himself writes in the Law[7] that 9
he did just this when, having chosen certain leaders from the tribes
of the sons of Israel, he left less important judgments to them,
retaining for himself alone the more important ones which concerned all of them; these judgments of more general relevance were
then applied by the leaders to their tribes, according to what was
appropriate for each particular tribe. Therefore it is better for man- 10
kind to be ruled by one person than by several, and thus by a
monarch who is the only ruler; and if this is better, then it is more
acceptable to God, since God always wills what is better. And since
when there are only two things being compared, the better *is* the
best, it follows that when the choice is between 'one' and 'more
than one', not only is the first of these more acceptable to God,
but it is entirely acceptable. It follows from this that mankind is in 11
its ideal state when it is ruled by one person; and thus monarchy
is necessary to the well-being of the world.

torial or 'equinoctial' zone (specifically, a region of SW Libya in North Africa).
Dante's knowledge of them came from Orosius, *Adversus Paganos historiarum libri
VII* (henceforth *Hist.*) 1, 2 and Albertus Magnus, *De natura loci* III, 5 (Alberti
Magni *Opera Omnia* V, Pars II, Monasterii Westfalorum in aedibus Aschendorff
1980). On the seven 'climates' or climatic zones into which medieval geographers
divided the northern hemisphere, and on the Scythians and Garamantes, see *Dict.*,
pp. 304–5 and 567.

[6] i.e. the relationship of the monarch to lesser princes is analogous to that of theoretical intellect to practical intellect, inasmuch as each supplies the general
(universal) principle which is applied to particular circumstances and then acted
on. The procedure in each case is analogous to a syllogistic argument in consisting
of three steps, the third of which 'concludes' the operation (with a deduction in
the case of a syllogism, an action in the other cases).

[7] Exodus 18, 13–26; Deuteronomy 1, 9–18.

XV

Again, I say that being, unity and goodness are related in a sequence, according to the fifth sense of the term 'priority'.[1] Being naturally comes before unity, and unity before goodness: perfect being is perfect unity, and perfect unity is perfect goodness; and the further removed something is from perfect being, the further
2 it is from being one and consequently from being good. Therefore in every species of thing the best is that which is perfectly one, as Aristotle says in the *Metaphysics*.[2] This is how it comes about that unity seems to be the root of what it is to be good, and plurality the root of what it is to be evil; that is why Pythagoras in his correlations placed unity on the side of goodness and plurality on the
3 side of evil, as is clear in the first book of the *Metaphysics*.[3] Hence it can be seen that to sin is nothing other than to spurn unity and move towards plurality; the Psalmist saw this when he said: 'From the fruit of the corn, the wine and the oil they have been multi-
4 plied.'[4] It is clear then that everything which is good is good for this reason: that it constitutes a unity. And since concord, in itself, is a good, it is clear that it consists in some unity as in its root.
5 What this root is will appear if we consider the nature or meaning of concord, for concord is a uniform movement of several wills; from this definition it is clear that unity of wills, which is what is signified by 'uniform movement', is the root of concord or indeed
6 is concord itself. For just as we would describe a number of clods of earth as being 'in concord' because of their all falling towards the centre of the world, and a number of flames as 'in concord' because of their all rising towards its circumference,[5] if they did this of their own free will; in the same way we describe a number of people as being 'in concord' when they move all together and of

---

[1] Aristotle, *Categories* 12 lists the five kinds of priority. Of the fifth kind he says: 'that which is in some way the cause of the other's existence might reasonably be called prior by nature' (14b 10–12); cf. *Summule* III, 30. See Boyde, *Dante Philomythes*, pp. 217–20, on 'oneness' and multiplicity.
[2] *Metaphysics* 10, 2 1053b 20–8; 1054a 9–13.
[3] *Metaphysics* 1, 5 986a 15–b 2.
[4] Psalms 4, 8 (AV 4, 7). The significance of this quotation is not immediately apparent; it becomes clearer if one bears in mind its context, which talks of the unity of God's light on the just man (contrasted with the multiplicity of material goods alluded to here).
[5] i.e. towards the heaven of the moon, the limit of the earth's atmosphere.

their own free will towards one thing which is in their wills formally,[6] just as there is one quality (heaviness) formally in the clods
of earth, and another (lightness) in the flames. For the capacity to 7
will is a potentiality, and its form is the image of good which is
perceived; and this form, just like other forms, is one in itself and
becomes multiple according to the multiplicity of the material which
receives it – just like soul, number and other forms which are found
in composites.

Having made these preliminary points in order to clarify the 8
proposition to be advanced for our purposes, we may reason as
follows: all concord depends on the unity which is in wills; mankind
in its ideal state represents a kind of concord; for just as one man
in his ideal state spiritually and physically is a kind of concord (and
the same holds true of a household, a city, and a kingdom), so is
the whole of mankind; thus the whole of mankind in its ideal state
depends on the unity which is in men's wills.[7] But this cannot be 9
unless there is one will which controls and directs all the others
towards one goal, since the wills of mortals require guidance on
account of the seductive pleasures of youth, as Aristotle teaches at
the end of the *Ethics*.[8] Nor can such a single will exist, unless there
is one ruler who rules over everybody, whose will can control and
guide all the other wills. Now if all the above conclusions[9] are true – 10
as they are – for mankind to be in its ideal state there must be a
monarch in the world, and consequently the well-being of the world
requires a monarchy.

---

[6] i.e. as 'form', as goal or objective (the meaning is clarified by the definition of
'form' [*forma*] in the next paragraph). The parallel between clods of earth and
men strikes us as strange because we are not used to language which applies
equally to animate and inanimate processes in nature, i.e. those which involve
consciousness and volition and those which do not. For Dante, as for Aristotle,
such language was normal.

[7] Aquinas *In Eth.* devotes Lecture VI on Book IX to a discussion of concord in
these terms.

[8] *Ethics* 10, 9 1179b 32f.

[9] i.e. not just the conclusions reached in this chapter, but *all* the conclusions reached
so far from ch. v on – the conclusions, as Bruno Nardi puts it, of 'eleven chapters
inspired by Aristotle's metaphysics, physics and ethics'. But the answer to the
question of where this monarchy is to be found does not come from Aristotle;
that answer is supplied by Virgil, and will provide the subject-matter of Book II.

xvi

All the arguments advanced so far are confirmed by a remarkable historical fact:[1] namely the state of humanity which the Son of God either awaited, or himself chose to bring about, when he was on the point of becoming man for the salvation of mankind. For if we review the ages and the dispositions of men from the fall of our first parents (which was the turning-point at which we went astray), we shall not find that there ever was peace throughout the world except under the immortal Augustus, when a perfect monarchy

2 existed. That mankind was then happy in the calm of universal peace is attested by all historians[2] and by famous poets; even the chronicler of Christ's gentleness[3] deigned to bear witness to it; and finally Paul called that most happy state 'the fullness of time'.[4] Truly that time was 'full', as were all temporal things, for no minis-

3 try to our happiness lacked its minister. What the state of the world has been since that seamless garment[5] was first rent by the talon of cupidity we can read about – would that we might not witness it.

4 O human race, how many storms and misfortunes and shipwrecks must toss you about while, transformed into a many-headed beast,[6]

5 you strive after conflicting things. You are sick in your intellects, both of them,[7] and in your affections; you do not nurture your higher intellect with inviolable principles, nor your lower intellect

[1] The arguments from philosophical principles (abstract, based in reason) which have been advanced up to this point are now shown to be confirmed by the facts of history (concrete, based in experience), leading to the impassioned conclusion of Book I: both these sources of knowledge and understanding are ignored by humanity, as is also the enlightenment that comes from the Scriptures, which speak directly to the human heart.

[2] Notably by Orosius, in whose view of world history the temporal coinciding of Christ's birth and peace under the rule of Augustus is the pivotal event; see *Hist.* 3, 8 and 6, 22 (and II, x, n. 7).

[3] i.e. Luke 2, 1. Luke does not talk of peace, but biblical exegetes assumed that unless there had been universal peace Augustus could not have issued a universal edict.

[4] Galatians 4, 4.

[5] Christ's seamless garment (John 19, 23) symbolizes the unity of the empire; the rending of the garment was effected, in Dante's eyes, by the donation of Constantine, an event whose significance will be examined in III, x (see n. 1). The expression had been used by Pope Boniface VIII in *Unam sanctam* to signify the indissoluble unity of the church.

[6] Cf. Revelation 12, 3 and 17, 9.

[7] i.e. theoretical and practical.

with the lessons of experience, nor your affections with the sweet-
ness of divine counsel, when it is breathed into you by the trumpet
of the holy spirit: 'Behold how good and how pleasant it is for
brethren to dwell together in unity.'[8]

---

[8] Psalms 132, 1 (AV 133, 1).

Book Two

i

'Why have the nations raged, and the peoples meditated vain things? The kings of the earth have arisen, and the princes have gathered together against the Lord and against his Christ. Let us burst their chains and cast their yoke from us.'[1]

2   When confronted with an unfamiliar phenomenon whose cause we do not comprehend we usually feel amazement; and equally, when we do understand the cause, we look down almost mockingly on those who continue to be amazed.[2] For my own part, I used once to be amazed that the Roman people had set themselves as rulers over the whole world without encountering any resistance, for I looked at the matter only in a superficial way and I thought that they had attained their supremacy not by right but only by

3   force of arms.[3] But when I penetrated with my mind's eye to the heart of the matter and understood through unmistakable signs that this was the work of divine providence, my amazement faded and a kind of scornful derision took its place, on seeing how the nations raged against the supremacy of the Roman people, on seeing the

---

[1] Psalms 2, 1–3.

[2] On the theme of amazement caused by a failure to recognize hidden causes (and specifically the role of providence in human history), cf. Boethius, *De consolatione philosophiae* 4, 5–6.

[3] As a young man Dante had accepted the Augustinian view of history which saw Roman supremacy as based on aggressive conquest (*De civ. Dei* IV, 4). Charles Davis in his classic study of Dante's vision of history and his understanding of the role of the Roman empire (*Dante and the Idea of Rome*, Oxford, 1957) examines the possible influence of Remigio de' Girolami on Dante's change of attitude (pp. 83–6).

peoples meditate vain things, as I myself once did; and I grieved
too that kings and princes should be united only in this one thing:
in opposing their Lord and his Anointed, the Roman prince. For 4
this reason I can cry out in defence of that glorious people and of
Caesar – mockingly, yet not without some feeling of grief – along
with him who cried out for the prince of Heaven: 'Why did the
nations rage, and the peoples meditate vain things? The kings of
the earth have arisen, and the princes have gathered together,
against their Lord and against his Christ.' But since natural love 5
does not allow scorn to last long, preferring (like the summer sun
which as it rises disperses the morning clouds and shines forth
radiantly) to cast scorn aside and to pour forth the light of correc-
tion, I too then, in order to break the chains of ignorance of kings
and princes such as these, and to show that the human race is free
of their yoke, shall take heart along with the most holy prophet, by
making my own the words of his which follow: 'Let us burst their
chains, and cast their yoke from us.' These two things will be suf- 6
ficiently accomplished when I have brought to completion the
second part of my present project and shown the truth of the question we are now considering. For showing that the Roman empire
is founded on right will not only disperse the fog of ignorance from
the eyes of kings and princes who usurp control of public affairs
for themselves, falsely believing the Roman people to have done the
same thing, but it will make all men understand that they are free
of the yoke of usurpers of this kind. The truth of the matter can 7
be revealed not only by the light of human reason but also by the
radiance of divine authority; when these two are in agreement,
heaven and earth must of necessity both give their assent. Relying 8
therefore on the faith of which I spoke earlier[4] and trusting in the
testimony of reason and authority, I proceed to resolve the second
question.

ii

Having sufficiently investigated the truth concerning the first question, within those limits the subject itself allows,[1] we must now

---

[4] Cf. *Mon.* I, i, 6.
[1] The Aristotelian principle that one must take into consideration the limits
imposed by the subject under discussion is repeatedly emphasized by Dante in
this book: cf. par. 7, and II, v, 6.

investigate the truth in relation to the second: that is, did the Roman people take on the dignity of empire by right? The starting-point of this investigation is to see what that truth is to which the arguments in this investigation can be referred back as to their own first

2 principle.[2] We must bear in mind then that, just as art is found at three levels, in the mind of the craftsman, in his instrument, and in the material shaped by his craft, so too we can consider nature at three levels. For nature is in the mind of the first mover, who is God; then in the heavens, as in the instrument by means of which

3 the image of eternal goodness is set forth in fluctuating matter. And just as, when the craftsman is perfect and his instrument is in excellent order, if a flaw occurs in the work of art[3] it is to be imputed exclusively to the material; in the same way, since God attains the highest perfection and his instrument (i.e. the heavens) cannot fall short of the perfection appropriate to it (as is clear from those things philosophy teaches us about the heavens), our conclusion is this: whatever flaws there are in earthly things are flaws due to the material of which they are constituted, and are no part of the intention of God the creator and the heavens; and whatever good there is in earthly things, since it cannot come from the material (which exists only as a potentiality), comes primarily from God the maker and secondarily from the heavens, which are the instrument of God's

4 handiwork, which is commonly called 'nature'. From what has been said it is now clear that right, being a good, exists firstly in the mind of God; and since everything which is in the mind of God *is* God (in conformity with that saying 'Whatever was made was life in him'[4]), and since God principally wills himself, it follows that right is willed by God as being something which is in him. And since in God will and what is willed are one and the same thing,

5 it further follows that divine will *is* right itself. And again it follows from this that in the created world[5] right is simply the image of

---

[2] The principle Dante seeks will be articulated in par. 6. The procedure exactly parallels that adopted in Book I.

[3] 'Art' [*ars*] is the capacity to make, produce, create, whether divine or human; 'work of art' here means any product of this capacity. On the role of the heavens as the instrument of God's art, see Boyde, *Dante Philomythes*, pp. 132–43.

[4] John 1, 3. (The AV interprets this phrase differently, with a break after 'was made', and a new sentence 'In him was life'.)

[5] Literally, 'in things' [*in rebus*]. The expression is used repeatedly as the argument evolves to indicate the created (material, sublunary) world in which natural laws

divine will; and thus it follows that whatever is not in harmony with divine will cannot be right, and whatever is in harmony with divine will is by that very fact right. And so to ask whether some- 6 thing happened by right, even though the words are different, is the same thing as asking whether it happened in accordance with God's will. Let us therefore formulate this principle: that what God wills in human society must be considered true and pure right. Besides it must be remembered that, as Aristotle teaches at the 7 beginning of the *Ethics*, certainty is not to be sought in the same way in every subject, but according as the nature of the subject-matter allows.[6] Therefore our arguments will be derived with sufficient rigour from the principle we have formulated, if we seek proof of the right of that glorious people in clear signs and the authoritative statements of wise men. For the will of God in itself 8 is indeed invisible; but the invisible things of God 'are clearly perceived by being understood through the things he has made'[7]; for although the seal is hidden, the wax stamped by the seal (hidden though it is) yields clear knowledge of it.[8] Nor is it a cause for amazement if God's will is to be sought through signs, since even the will of a human being is discernible to the outside world only through signs.[9]

iii

On this question I therefore affirm that it was by right, and not by usurping, that the Roman people took on the office of the monarch (which is called 'empire') over all men. This can be proved firstly 2 as follows: it is appropriate that the noblest race should rule over

operate and by which human experience is defined. The emphasis will vary according to context, depending on whether Dante is talking about the workings of nature, or human endeavour, or both (as here).

[6] *Ethics* I, 3 1094b 23–5 and 7 1098a 25–8 (see n. 1).
[7] Romans I, 20.
[8] The wax-and-seal metaphor for the relation of the created world to God, implicit from the opening sentence of the treatise, now becomes explicit, and provides the key to the argument developed in Book II, which will examine events in human history which enable us to perceive God's will; see *Mon.* I, viii, n. 1.
[9] An individual knows his own will through introspection, but no human being has access to another's mind. This idea also will be applied to the interpretation of Roman history in ch. v (par. 6), and will be developed in the remainder of that chapter.

all the others; the Roman people was the noblest; therefore it was
3 appropriate that they should rule over all the others. The major
premiss is proved by an argument from reason: for since 'honour
is the reward for virtue'[1] and every position of authority is an
honour, every position of authority is the reward of virtue. But we
know that men become noble through virtue, either their own virtue
4 or that of their forebears. For 'nobility is virtue and ancient wealth',
as Aristotle says in the *Politics*;[2] and according to Juvenal:

> nobility of mind is the sole and only virtue.[3]

These two sayings refer to two kinds of nobility, i.e. a man's own
nobility and that of his ancestors. Therefore the reward of a position
of authority is appropriate to the noble by reason of the cause of
5 their nobility.[4] And since rewards should be commensurate with
deserts, as we read in the words of the Gospel: 'With the same
measure you have applied to others you will be measured',[5] it is
appropriate that the most noble should have the highest position
6 of authority over others. The minor premiss[6] is supported by the
testimony of the ancients; for our divine poet Virgil bears witness
throughout the whole of the *Aeneid*, to his everlasting memory, that
the father of the Roman people was that most glorious king Aeneas;
and Titus Livy, the illustrious chronicler of Roman deeds, confirms
this in the first part of his book,[7] which takes as its starting-point

---

[1] Aristotle, *Ethics* 4, 3 1123b 35.

[2] *Politics* 4, 8 1294a 21–2.

[3] *Satires* 8, 20. The line is slightly different in modern critical editions of the text.
Dante may be quoting from memory, as he seems to do elsewhere; see n. 8; II,
vii, n. 17; II, ix, n. 6.

[4] The cause of nobility is virtue, therefore if a position of authority [*prelatio*] is due
to virtue it will be due to the noble.

[5] Matthew 7, 2; Luke 6, 38.

[6] The minor premiss [*subassumptam*] is that 'the Roman people were the noblest'.
The argument developed in this chapter consists of proving that the content of
the syllogism enunciated in par. 2 is true. The major premiss is proved in pars.
3–5; the minor premiss occupies the remainder of the chapter: pars. 6–16 establish
the nobility of Aeneas and hence of the Romans, using the key testimony of
Virgil, the principal witness to Rome's greatness, corroborated by others; par. 17
recapitulates, and reminds us, in case we have lost the thread during this extended
review of the evidence, that it bears on the proof of the minor premiss [*ad evi-
dentiam subassumpte*].

[7] *Ab urbe condita* 1, 1, 11. It is uncertain whether Dante had a firsthand knowledge
of Livy. The evidence is exhaustively reviewed by A. Martina in *Livio, ED* III,
pp. 673–7.

the capture of Troy. It would be beyond me to give a full account 7
of just how noble this supremely victorious and supremely dutiful
father was, taking into account not only his own virtue but that of
his forebears and his wives, whose nobility flowed into him by hereditary right: 'but I shall trace the main outlines of the facts'.[8]

Now as far as his own nobility is concerned, we must listen to our 8
poet when in the first book he introduces Ileoneus as he petitions in
this manner:

> Aeneas was our king; no man more just
> In piety, nor greater in war and arms.[9]

Let us listen to him too in the sixth book, when he speaks of the 9
dead Misenus, who had served Hector in battle and who after Hector's death had entered the service of Aeneas; he says that Misenus
'followed no less a hero',[10] comparing Aeneas with Hector, whom
Homer glorifies above all others, as Aristotle relates in that book of
the *Ethics* which deals with behaviour to be avoided.[11] As far as 10
hereditary nobility is concerned, we find that each of the three
regions into which the world is divided[12] made him noble, both
through his ancestors and through his wives. For Asia did so
through his more immediate forebears, such as Assaracus and the
others who ruled over Phrygia, a region of Asia; hence our poet
says in the third book:

> After the Gods saw fit to overthrow
> The might of Asia and Priam's guiltless race.[13]

Europe did so with his most ancient male forebear, i.e. Dardanus; 11
Africa did so too with his most ancient female forebear Electra,
daughter of King Atlas of great renown; our poet bears witness
concerning both of them in his eighth book, where Aeneas speaks
in these words to Evander:

---

[8] *Aeneid* I, 342. Again Dante is either quoting from memory, or from a text with
the variant reading *vestigia* instead of *fastigia*.
[9] *ibid.* I, 544–5.
[10] *ibid.* VI, 170.
[11] *Ethics* 7, 1 1145a 20–3.
[12] This tripartite division of the world derives from Orosius, *Hist.* I, I; cf. also
Alberti Magni *De natura loci*, Tract. 3 Cap. 5 [*De distinctione trium partium orbis:
Asiae, Europae et Africae*]; and see *Mon.* I, xiv, n. 5.
[13] *Aeneid* III, 1–2.

> Dardanus,
> First father and founder of the city of Troy,
> Born of Electra, as the Greeks maintain,
> Comes to the Teucrians; mighty Atlas begat her,
> Who bears the spheres of heaven on his shoulders.[14]

12 That Dardanus was of European birth our bard[15] proclaims in the third book:

> There is a land the Greeks call Hesperia,
> Ancient, mighty in arms and fertile soil.
> Oenotrians lived there; a later generation
> Has called the nation Italy after their leader:
> This is our homeland; Dardanus was born here.[16]

13 That Atlas came from Africa is confirmed by the mountain there which bears his name. Orosius in his description of the world tells us it is in Africa in these words: 'Its furthest boundary is Mount Atlas and the islands they call Fortunate' ('its' meaning 'Africa's', because he is talking about Africa).[17]

14   In similar fashion I find that he was also made noble by marriage. For his first wife, Creusa, the daughter of king Priam, was from Asia, as may be gathered from what was said earlier. And that she was his wife our poet bears witness in his third book, where Andromache questions Aeneas as a father about his son Ascanius in this way:

> What of your boy Ascanius,
> Whom Creusa bore when Troy was smouldering?
> Is he alive and does he breathe earth's air?[18]

15 His second wife was Dido, queen and mother of the Carthaginians in Africa; and that she was his wife our bard proclaims in the fourth book, for he says there of Dido:

---

[14] *ibid.* VIII, 134–7.

[15] The word 'bard' [*vates*] underlines Virgil's prophetic function, reiterated in the verb [*vaticinatur*] used in par. 15.

[16] *Aeneid* III, 163–7.

[17] *Hist.* I, 2. Mount Atlas is on the NW coast of Africa; the Fortunate Isles are Madeira and the Canaries.

[18] *Aeneid* III, 339–40. Line 340 [*quem tibi iam Troia..?*] is the only incomplete line in the *Aeneid* where the sense is incomplete (Servius *ad Aen.* III, 340 draws attention to the incomplete sense). In medieval manuscripts the lacuna is occasionally filled as Dante fills it here (inappropriately, as Ascanius was born long before the destruction of Troy).

Dido no longer thinks of a secret love:
She calls it marriage; this name conceals her sin.[19]

The third was Lavinia, mother of the Albans and the Romans, the 16
daughter of King Latinus and his heir as well, if our poet is to be
believed in his last book, where he introduces the defeated Turnus
making supplication to Aeneas in these words:

You have won; the Ausonians have seen
The vanquished man stretch forth his upturned hands:
Lavinia is your wife.[20]

This last wife was from Italy, the most noble region of Europe. When 17
these facts in support of the minor premiss are borne in mind, who is
not satisfied that the father of the Roman people, and as a consequence
that people itself, was the noblest in the world? Or who will fail to
recognize divine predestination in that double confluence of blood[21]
from every part of the world into a single man?

iv

Moreover whatever is brought to full realization with the aid of
miracles is willed by God, and consequently comes about by right.
And it is clear that this is true because, as Thomas says in his
third book *Contra Gentiles*,[1] a miracle is something done by divine
intervention outside the normal order in our created world.[2] And 2
thus he proves that only God has the power to perform miracles;
and this is corroborated by the authority of Moses, where he tells
how, when confronted with the gnats, Pharaoh's magicians, using
natural principles in the service of their arts and failing, said: 'This
is the finger of God.'[3] Now if a miracle is a direct action by the 3

---

[19] *Aeneid* IV, 171-2.
[20] *ibid.* XII, 936-7.
[21] i.e. from ancestors and wives.
[1] Aquinas, *Contra Gentiles* 3, 101-2.
[2] See II, ii, n. 5.
[3] *Exodus* 8, 16-19. The reference is to the third of the plagues visited on Pharaoh,
the plague of *scinifes*: 'a kind of stinging insect' (Lewis and Short), 'lice' in the
Authorised Version, 'mosquitoes' in the New Jerusalem Bible, 'maggots' in the
New English Bible, 'gnats' in the New Revised Standard Version and the Good
News Bible. Orosius, *Hist.* 7, 26, reviewing the plagues of Egypt and drawing a
parallel with ten calamities which befell Rome, describes *scinifes*, with the air
of one speaking from personal experience, as 'very small and troublesome flies
[*musculas. . .parvissimas ac saevissimas*], which often in midsummer gather in dense

First Cause without the mediation of secondary agents – as Thomas himself proves with sufficient rigour in the book just cited[4] – then when a portent takes place in favour of something, it is wicked to say that the thing so favoured is not ordained by
4 God as something pleasing to him. It is therefore holy[5] to acknowledge the converse: the Roman empire was aided by the help of miracles to achieve supremacy; therefore it was willed by
5 God; and consequently it was and is founded on right. That God performed miracles so that the Roman empire might be supreme is confirmed by the testimony of illustrious authors. For Livy tells in the first part of his work[6] that in the time of Numa Pompilius, the second king of the Romans, a shield fell from heaven into God's chosen city as he was sacrificing according to
6 the pagan rite. Lucan recalls this miracle in the ninth book of the *Pharsalia* where he describes the incredible force of the South wind to which Libya is exposed; for he says:

> No doubt the shields,
> Which chosen youths bore on patrician necks,
> Fell before Numa as he sacrificed;
> The South wind or the North had robbed their bearers
> Of shields which now are ours.[7]

7 When the Gauls, having captured the rest of the city, and trusting to the shadows of night, secretly stole up to the Capitol (whose fall would have meant the annihilation of the very name of Rome), a goose never seen there before cried warning that the Gauls had come and roused the guardians to defend the Capitol (Livy and
8 many other illustrious writers concur in their testimony).[8] Our poet recalled this incident when he described Aeneas' shield in the eighth book; for he writes as follows:

swarms about filthy places and as they buzz around settle down and lodge in men's hair and on the hides of cattle, stinging their victims and causing acute pain'.
[4] *Contra Gentiles* 3, 99.
[5] If it is impious to assert an untruth, then logically it is holy to assert its opposite.
[6] *Ab urbe condita* 1, 20, 4; 5, 54, 7.
[7] *Pharsalia* IX, 477–80. The story of the holy shields is told at greater length by Ovid, *Fasti* III, 259–398 and mentioned by Virgil, *Aeneid* VIII, 664.
[8] *Ab urbe condita* 5, 47, 4–5. Livy speaks of more than one goose, but Virgil's testimony is decisive. Other writers include St Augustine, *De civ. Dei* 2, 22 and 3, 8. Orosius, *Hist.* 2, 19, does not mention the geese.

At the top before the temple stood
Manlius, guardian of the Tarpeian rock,
And held the lofty heights of the Capitol;
The new-built palace was rough with Romulus' thatch.
Here flying through the golden colonnades
A silver goose cried warning that the Gauls
Were at the gate.[9]

And when the nobility of Rome, under siege by Hannibal, was fallen 9 so low that all that remained to complete the destruction of Roman might was the onslaught of the Carthaginians on the city, the victors were unable to complete their victory because of a sudden unbearably violent hailstorm which threw them into confusion. Livy recounts this among other events in the Punic wars.[10] And when, 10 during the siege of Porsenna, Cloelia – a woman, and a prisoner – broke her chains and swam across the Tiber with the miraculous help of God, as almost all Roman historians relate to her glory, was her crossing not miraculous?[11] It was utterly fitting that he who 11 ordained all things from eternity in harmonious order should operate in this manner: that just as he would, when visible,[12] perform miracles as testimony for invisible things, so he should, while still invisible,[13] perform them as testimony for visible things.[14]

V

Moreover, whoever has the good of the community as his goal has the achievement of right as his goal. That the one necessarily follows from the other can be shown in this way: right is a relationship[1] between one individual and another in respect of things and people; when it is respected it preserves human society and when it is viol-

---

[9] *Aeneid* VIII, 652–6.
[10] *Ab urbe condita* 26, 11, 1–3; Orosius, *Hist.* 4, 17.
[11] Cloelia is mentioned by Livy, *Ab urbe condita* 2, 13, 6–11; Orosius, *Hist.* 2, 5; and on the shield in *Aeneid* VIII, 651 (only Virgil speaks of broken chains [*vinclis. . .ruptis*]).
[12] i.e. when made man in the person of Christ.
[13] i.e. before the incarnation.
[14] In treating these events as miracles Dante is not necessarily following his sources (Augustine, for example, is scathing about the role of the geese in saving Rome, see Introduction, pp. xviii–xix).
[1] Cf. Aristotle, *Ethics* 5, 5–6.

ated it destroys it. For the description of it given in the *Digests*[2] does not say what right is, but describes it in terms of its practical
2 application. If therefore our definition correctly embraces both the essence and the purpose of right, and if the goal of any society is the common good of its members, it necessarily follows that the purpose of every right is the common good; and it is impossible that there can be a right which does not aim at the common good. Hence Cicero is correct when he says in the *De inventione*[3] that laws
3 are always to be interpreted for the benefit of the community. For if laws are not framed for the benefit of those who are subject to the law, they are laws in name only, but in reality they cannot be laws; for laws must bind men together for their mutual benefit. For this reason Seneca speaks appositely of the law when he says in *De*
4 *quatuor virtutibus* that 'law is the bond of human society'.[4] Thus it is clear that whoever has the good of the community as his goal has the achievement of right as his goal. Therefore if the Romans had the good of the community as their goal, it will be true to say
5 that the achievement of right was their goal. That the Roman people in conquering the world did have the good of which we have spoken as their goal is shown by their deeds, for, having repressed all greed (which is always harmful to the community) and cherishing universal peace and freedom, that holy, dutiful and glorious people can be seen to have disregarded personal advantage in order to promote the public interest for the benefit of mankind.[5] Thus with good reason it was written: 'The Roman empire is born of the fountain-head of piety.'[6]

---

[2] The *Digests* are a compilation of extracts from the writings of the jurists assembled at the instigation of Justinian in 533. The description given there was not a rigorous definition; see P. Fiorelli, 'Sul senso del diritto nella *Monarchia*', in *Letture classensi* 16, Ravenna 1987, pp. 79–97.

[3] *De inventione* 1, 38 (Dante uses the title *Prima rethorica*).

[4] The *De quatuor virtutibus* (not in fact by Seneca) is now attributed to S. Martin of Dumio, Archbishop of Braga in Portugal (d. 580).

[5] This interpretation of Roman history as the triumph of civic unselfishness is, as noted (see II, 1, n. 3 and Introduction, p. xix), consciously opposed to St Augustine, who regarded Roman conquests through aggressive war as acts of brigandage [*magna latrocinia*].

[6] This phrase is used in the *Legenda aurea* by Jacopo da Varagine à propos of Constantine's refusal to attempt a cure for his leprosy by bathing in the blood of 3000 slaughtered children, as he had been counselled.

But since it is only through external signs that anything about 6
the intentions of all free agents is revealed to the outside world,[7]
and since our arguments must be sought in accordance with our
subject matter, as we have already said,[8] it will suffice for our purposes if we discover indubitable signs revealing the intention of the
Roman people both in its collegiate bodies and in individual citizens. As for its collegiate bodies,[9] which seem in some sense to 7
function as a bond between individuals and the community, the
sole authority of Cicero in the *De officiis* is sufficient: 'So long as
the power of the state was exercised through acts of service and
not of oppression, wars were waged either on behalf of our allies
or to safeguard our supremacy, and the consequences of wars were
mild or else unavoidable; the senate was a haven and a refuge for
kings, peoples and nations; both our magistrates and our military
chiefs strove to win praise for this above all, for defending the provinces and our allies justly and loyally. Thus "protection" of the
world might be a more appropriate term than "domination".'[10]
These are Cicero's words.

As for individuals, I shall proceed with brief sketches.[11] Are they 8
not to be described as having aimed at the common good who strove
to increase the public good with toil, with poverty, with exile, with
the loss of their children, the loss of their limbs, even the loss of
their lives? Did not the great Cincinnatus leave us a holy example 9
of freely relinquishing his high office when his term came to an
end? Taken from his plough to become dictator, as Livy relates,[12]
after his victory and his triumph he handed back the sceptre of
office to the consuls and went back of his own free will to toil at
the plough-handle behind his oxen. Cicero indeed, arguing against 10
Epicurus in the *De fine bonorum*, recalls this act of public service

---

[7] Cf. *Mon.* II, ii, 8.
[8] See notes 1 and 6 to *Mon.* II, ii.
[9] Pre-eminently the Roman senate.
[10] *De officiis* 2, 8, 26–7. Again Dante quotes the text in a form which has minor
divergences from modern editions.
[11] Most of the Roman heroes celebrated in the paragraphs which follow are mentioned by Augustine, *De civ. Dei* 5, 18, where their actions are interpreted very
differently, see e.g. n. 21.
[12] *Ab urbe condita* 3, 26f.; Orosius, *Hist.* 2, 12. Neither Livy nor Orosius talks of a
return to the plough, though Orosius mentions the plough-handle ('holding victory in his hands as he had held the handle of his plough. . .').

approvingly: 'And thus our ancestors led the great Cincinnatus from
11 the plough to make him dictator.'[13] Did not Fabritius give us a lofty
example of resisting avarice when, poor as he was, out of loyalty to
the republic he scorned the great sum of gold which was offered
him – scorned it and spurned it with disdain, uttering words in
keeping with his character? The memory of this incident too is
confirmed by our poet in his sixth book when he said:

> Fabritius, a great man in his poverty.[14]

12 Did not Camillus give us a memorable example of putting the law
before personal advantage? Condemned to exile, according to
Livy,[15] after he had freed his besieged country and returned the
Roman spoils to Rome, he left the holy city although the whole
populace clamoured against his going, and he did not return until
permission to come back to Rome was brought to him by authority
of the senate. And our poet commends this great spirit in his sixth
book when he says:

> Camillus bringing back the standards.[16]

13 Did not the first Brutus teach us that not just all other people but
our own children must take second place to freedom of the fatherland? Livy[17] says that when he was consul he condemned his own
sons to death for conspiring with the enemy. His glory lives on in
our poet's sixth book when he says of him:

> In fair freedom's name
> The father condemned to death his own two sons
> Plotting new wars.[18]

14 What did Mutius not teach us to dare for the fatherland when he
attacked Porsenna, who was off his guard, and then watched his
own hand which had missed its mark burn in the fire with the same
expression on his face as if he saw an enemy being tortured? Even

---

[13] *De finibus* 2, 4, 12.

[14] *Aeneid* VI, 843–4.

[15] *Ab urbe condita* 5, 46f. Livy makes no mention of a second exile; the source seems
to be Servius *ad Aen.* VI, 825.

[16] *Aeneid* VI, 825.

[17] *Ab urbe condita* 2, 5.

[18] *Aeneid* VI, 820–1.

Livy expresses amazement as he reports this incident.[19] Now add 15
to their number those most holy victims, the Decii, who laid down
their lives dedicated to the salvation of the community, as Livy
relates to their glory, not in terms worthy of them but as best he
can;[20] and that sacrifice (words cannot express it)[21] of the most stern
guardian of liberty, Marcus Cato. The former for the deliverance
of their fatherland did not recoil from the shadows of death; the
latter, in order to set the world afire with love of freedom, showed
the value of freedom when he preferred to die a free man rather
than remain alive without freedom. The great renown of all these 16
men lives on in the words of Cicero. For Cicero says this of the
Decii in the *De fine bonorum*: 'When Publius Decius, first in that
family to be consul, offered himself up and charged on his horse
at full speed into the thick of the Latin ranks, surely he had no
thought of personal pleasure, or where or when he might seize it;
for he knew that he was about to die, and sought out death with
more passionate eagerness than Epicurus thinks we should devote
to seeking pleasure. But had this action of his not been praised
with good reason, his son would not have imitated it in his fourth
consulship; nor would his son's son in his turn, when he was consul
in the war against Pyrrhus, have fallen in battle and offered himself
to the state as the third victim from succeeding generations of the
same family.'[22] In the *De officiis* he says of Cato: 'For the situation 17
of Marcus Cato was no different from that of the others who surren-
dered to Caesar in Africa. Yet if the others had killed themselves
it would perhaps have been accounted a fault in them, because their
lives were less austere and their habits more relaxed; but since
nature had bestowed on Cato an austerity beyond belief, and he
had strengthened it with unfailing constancy, and had always per-
sisted in any resolve or plan he had undertaken, it was fitting that
he should die rather than set eyes on the face of the tyrant.'[23]

---

[19] *Ab urbe condita* 2, 12. Mutius' plan to assassinate Porsenna misfired when he
killed Porsenna's secretary by mistake instead of the enemy leader himself. When
captured, in order to show the fearlessness and resolve of the Romans, Mutius
plunged his own hand into the fire and watched expressionless as it burned.

[20] *ibid.* 8, 9 and 10, 28.

[21] Cf. Augustine's unenthusiastic account of Cato in *De civ. Dei* 1, 23.

[22] *De finibus* 2, 19, 61.

[23] *De officiis* 1, 31, 112.

18 Thus two things have been explained; the first is that whoever has the good of the community as his goal has the achievement of right as his goal; the other is that the Roman people in conquering
19 the world had the public good as their goal. Now it may be argued for our purposes as follows: whoever has right as his goal proceeds with right; the Roman people subjecting the world to its rule had right as its goal, as has been clearly demonstrated by what has been said already in this chapter; therefore the Roman people subjecting the world to its rule did this in accordance with right, and as a
20 consequence took upon itself the dignity of empire by right. For this conclusion to be inferred from premises which are all clear, the following statement must be clarified: that whoever has right as his goal proceeds with right. To clarify this it must be borne in mind that each and every thing exists for some purpose; otherwise
21 it would be useless, which is not possible, as we said earlier.[24] And in the same way that each thing exists for its own particular purpose,[25] so too each purpose has some thing of which it is the purpose; and so it is impossible strictly speaking for any two things, in so far as they *are* two, to have the same purpose; for the same inadmissible conclusion would follow, i.e. that one of them would
22 exist in vain. Now since there exists a purpose of right – as we have already explained – then having postulated the purpose it becomes necessary to postulate right, since the purpose is an intrinsic and necessary effect of right. And since in any relationship of consequentiality it is impossible to have the antecedent without the consequent,[26] as for example one cannot have 'man' without 'animal' – as is clear if one affirms the first while denying the second[27] – it is impossible to seek the purpose of right without right, since each and every thing is related to its own particular purpose as consequent is to antecedent; e.g. it is impossible to have a healthy

[24] Cf. *Mon.* I, iii, 3.
[25] Its own end or purpose can be achieved by that thing alone and by nothing else; hence (par. 22) the purpose stands to the thing in the relationship of antecedent to consequent (see n. 26).
[26] The relationship of antecedent to consequent is one of necessary implication; it can exist between concepts (e.g. 'man' and 'animal', as Dante says here) and between propositions, see II, x, n. 4. The two are logically inseparable: 'man' necessarily, by definition, implies 'animal'.
[27] i.e. if one tries to conceive of 'man' without the notion of 'animal' (by making an affirmative statement 'X is a man' along with a negative statement 'X is not an animal'), the necessary relationship between the two concepts will be apparent.

condition of the limbs without having good health. From this it is 23
quite apparent that one who seeks the purpose of right must seek
it with right; nor is this invalidated by the objection which is cus-
tomarily based on Aristotle's words where he discusses 'eubulia'.[28]
For Aristotle says: 'Yet it is possible to attain even good by a false
syllogism: to attain what one ought, but not by the right means,
the middle term being false.'[29] For if a true conclusion is in some 24
way arrived at from false premisses,[30] this happens by accident, inasmuch as the truth is introduced in the words of the conclusion; for
in itself truth never follows from false premisses, but words expressing truth may well follow from words which express falsehood. And 25
the same is true in actions;[31] for although the thief may help the
poor man with the proceeds of his thieving, nonetheless we cannot
call this alms-giving, although it is an action which would be alms-
giving if it were done with his own property.[32] The same is true of 26
the purpose of right, because if anything were to be obtained as the
purpose of this right but without right, that thing would be the
purpose of right (i.e. the common good) in the same way as the
giving of stolen goods is alms-giving; and so, since in our proposition we are speaking of the purpose of right as it really is, not
just as it appears to be, the objection has no force. The point we
were inquiring into is thus quite clear.

vi

Besides it is right to preserve what nature has ordained, for nature
in the measures it takes is no less provident than man; if it were
so, the effect would surpass its cause in goodness, which is impossible. But we see that in the setting up of collegiate bodies it is not 2

[28] i.e. excellence of deliberation, right judgment [*rectitudo consilii...per quam aliquis
adipiscitur bonum finem*, Aquinas *In Eth.*, Lecture VIII on Book VI: the entire
lecture is devoted to *eubulia*, which is discussed by Aristotle in *Ethics* 6, 9].
[29] *Ethics* 6, 9 1142b 22–4. Dante is anticipating a possible objection, namely that the
Roman people achieved the right goal by chance, not by right.
[30] Aristotle details the ways in which a true conclusion can be drawn from false
premisses in *Prior Analytics* 2, 2–4. Such conclusions are true in respect of the
fact, not the reason.
[31] The parallel between the procedures involved in taking action and in arguing
logically to a conclusion had already been spelled out in *Mon.* I, xiv, 7.
[32] This same example of theft and alms-giving is used by Aquinas to illustrate the
point in his commentary on this passage of the *Ethics*, see n. 28.

only the relationship of the members to one another which is taken into account by the founder, but also their capacity to exercise office; and this is to take into account the limits of right within the collegiate body, that is to say in the way it is structured; for right does not extend beyond the capacity to exercise it. Now nature is

3 no less provident than this in its ordering of things.[1] From this it is clear that nature orders things according to their capacities, and this taking into account of their capacities is the basis of right established by nature in the created world.[2] From this it follows that the natural order in the created world cannot be maintained without right, since the basis of right is inseparably bound up with that order: the preservation of that order is therefore necessarily right.

4 The Roman people were ordained by nature to rule; and this can be shown as follows: just as a craftsman would never achieve artistic perfection if he aimed only at the final form and paid no heed to the means by which that form was to be achieved, so too nature would fail if it aimed only at the universal form of divine likeness in the universe, yet neglected the means to achieve it; but nature is never less than perfect, since it is the work of divine intelligence:[3] therefore it wills all the means through which it achieves the fulfil-

5 ling of its intention. Since therefore the goal of the human race is itself a necessary means to achieving the universal goal of nature, it is necessary that nature wills it. For this reason Aristotle in the second book of the *Physics*[4] rightly shows that nature always acts

6 with an end in view. And since nature cannot achieve this end by means of one person alone, since there are many functions necessarily involved in it, and these functions require a vast number of people to carry them out, it is necessary for nature to produce a vast number of people fitted to different functions:[5] as well as celestial influences, the qualities and characteristics of regions here below

---

[1] In human institutions the power conferred on an individual elected to office will reflect that person's abilities; in the natural world power and aptitude are correlated in the same way, for it is unthinkable that nature should be less careful in its provisions than human beings.

[2] See *Mon.* II, ii, n. 5.

[3] Cf. *Mon.* II, ii, 3.

[4] *Physics* 2, 2 194a 28–31.

[5] The need for human diversity of which Aristotle speaks as a practical social and political necessity is here given a teleological explanation.

on earth make a large contribution to this.[6] This is why we see that 7
not just certain individuals, but certain peoples are born fitted to
rule, and certain others to be ruled and to serve, as Aristotle affirms
in the *Politics*;[7] and, as he says, it is not only expedient but actually
just that such people should be ruled, even if force has to be used
to bring this about. If this is the way things are, there is no doubt 8
that nature ordained a place and a nation to exercise universal rule
in the world: otherwise she would have failed in her provisions,
which is impossible. From what has been said above and what will
be said below it is clear enough which place that was and which
nation: it was Rome and her citizens, that is to say her people. Our 9
poet too touched on this perceptively in his sixth book, when he
introduces Anchises making this prophetic prediction to Aeneas,
the father of the Romans:

> That others shall beat out the breathing bronze
> More delicately, I can well believe,
> And draw forth living features from the marble,
> Plead causes better, trace movements of the heavens
> With pointers, tell the rising of the stars.
> Roman, remember to rule over nations.
> Your arts shall be: to impose the ways of peace,
> Spare subject peoples, and subdue the proud.[8]

He touches on the location of the place perceptively in the fourth 10
book, when he introduces Jove speaking of Aeneas to Mercury in
this manner:

> Not such a son did his fair mother promise,
> Nor for this saved him twice from Grecian arms;
> But that he might rule over Italy,
> Pregnant with empire, clamouring for war.[9]

These arguments are sufficient to convince us that the Roman 11
people were ordained by nature to rule; therefore the Roman people
by conquering the world came to empire by right.

[6] On the influence of geography on human diversification, cf. *Mon.* I, xiv, 6; on
the influence of astronomy, see Boyde, *Dante Philomythes*, p. 255.
[7] *Politics* I, 5 1254a 21–3; 1255a 1–2; 6 1255b 5–9 (though Aristotle is talking about
individuals rather than races or nations).
[8] *Aeneid* VI, 847–53.
[9] *ibid.* IV, 227–30.

vii

In order to get a secure grasp of the truth of our question it must moreover be borne in mind that divine judgment in earthly affairs is sometimes revealed to men, and sometimes it remains hidden.

2 Now there are two ways in which it can be revealed, i.e. by reason and by faith. For there are some judgments of God which human reason can arrive at by its own unaided efforts, such as this: that a man should sacrifice himself to save his country; for if the part should put itself at risk for the sake of the whole, then since man is a part of his community, as Aristotle says in the *Politics*,[1] then a man should sacrifice himself for his country, as a lesser good for a

3 greater. And so Aristotle says in the *Ethics*: 'though it is worthwhile to attain the good merely for one man, it is finer and more godlike to attain it for a people or a community'.[2] And this is God's judgment; otherwise human reason in its right judgment would not be in harmony with nature's intention, which is impossible. Then there are

4 some judgments of God to which human reason, even if it cannot arrive at them by its own unaided efforts, can nonetheless be raised with the help of faith in those things which are said to us in the Scriptures; such as this: that no one can be saved without faith (assuming that he has never heard anything of Christ), no matter how perfectly endowed he might be in the moral and intellectual

5 virtues[3] in respect both of his character and his behaviour. For human reason cannot see this to be just by its own powers, but with the aid of faith it can. For it is written to the *Hebrews*: 'It is impossible to please God without faith';[4] and in *Leviticus*: 'Any man of the house of Israel who shall kill an ox or lamb or goat in the camp or outside the camp, and shall not bring it to the door of the

6 tabernacle as an offering to the Lord, shall be guilty of blood.'[5] The door of the tabernacle is a figure of Christ, who is the doorway to the eternal assembly, as can be gathered from the Gospel; the killing

---

[1] *Politics* 1, 2 1253a 25–39.
[2] *Ethics* 1, 2 1094b 9–11.
[3] The distinction between the moral and intellectual virtues is made by Aristotle, *Ethics* 1, 13 1103a 4–10: the moral virtues are analysed in Books 2–5, the intellectual virtues in Book 6.
[4] Hebrews 11, 6.
[5] Leviticus 17, 3.

of animals symbolizes human actions.[6] But that judgment of God 7
is hidden which human reason arrives at neither through the law
of nature, nor the law of the scriptures, but occasionally by special
grace. This can happen in several ways, sometimes by direct revelation, and sometimes being revealed through some kind of putting-
to-the-test. There are two ways in which it can happen by direct 8
revelation: either by a spontaneous act of God, or by God in
response to prayer.[7] By a spontaneous act of God there are two
ways: either openly or through a sign; openly, as when the judgment
against Saul was revealed to Samuel;[8] by a sign, as when what God
willed regarding the liberation of the children of Israel was revealed
to Pharaoh through a sign.[9] It can be a response to prayer, as they
knew who said in the second book of *Chronicles*: 'When we do not
know what we should do, this course alone is left us: that we should
turn our eyes to Thee.'[10] There are two ways in which it can be 9
revealed through a putting-to-the-test: either by lot or through a
contest; for the word *certare* ('to decide something by a contest')
derives from *certum facere* ('to make certain').[11] God's judgment is
sometimes revealed to men by lot, as in the substitution of Matthias
in the *Acts of the Apostles*.[12] God's judgment can be revealed by a
contest in two ways: either by a clash of strength, as happens in
combat between two champions, who are called prize-fighters, or
through competition among a number of people who vie with one
another to reach an agreed goal, as happens in a race between athletes competing to reach the finishing-line first. The first of these 10
ways was prefigured among the pagans in that famous fight between
Hercules and Antaeus, which Lucan recalls in the fourth book of

---

[6] Commentators have not identified a source for the figural interpretation of this
passage from Leviticus, which may well be Dante's own; on Christ as *ostium* cf.
John 10, 9 [*ego sum ostium; per me si quis introierit salvabitur*, 'I am the door: by
me if any man enter in, he shall be saved'].

[7] The distinctions are sketched here with extreme conciseness, almost as a series
of notes with illustrative examples, the point being to clarify the two particular
forms of revelation which Dante will invite us to recognize as operating in the
course of Roman history.

[8] 1 Regum 15 (AV 1 Samuel).

[9] Exodus 7.

[10] 2 Chronicles 20, 12.

[11] The etymology Dante gives is false (*certus* comes from *cerno*, not *certo*).

[12] Acts 1, 26. Matthias was chosen to take the place of Judas among the apostles by
drawing lots.

the *Pharsalia*[13] and Ovid in the ninth book of the *Metamorphoses*;[14] the second was prefigured among those same pagans by the race between Atalanta and Hippomene in the tenth book of the *Meta-*
11 *morphoses*.[15] Nor should we overlook the fact that in these two kinds of contest different rules apply: in the first the contestants can obstruct each other quite legitimately (for instance prize-fighters), whereas in the second this is not allowed; for runners must not obstruct one another – although our poet seems to have thought differently in his fifth book, when he had Eurialus win the prize.[16]
12 So that Cicero did better to forbid this, in the third book of the *De officiis*, following the opinion of Chrysippus; for he says as follows: 'With his customary aptness Chrysippus says: "When a man races in the arena he must exert himself and strive his hardest to win; he must not in any way obstruct his fellow-competitor."'[17]
13 Having made these distinctions in this chapter, we can take two lines of argument which serve our purpose: one from the competition between runners, the other from the contest between prize-fighters. I shall develop these arguments in the chapters which now directly follow.[18]

viii

Thus that people who won the race to rule the world against all competition did so by divine decree. For since the resolving of a universal dispute is of greater concern to God than the resolving of a limited dispute, and in some limited disputes we seek to know divine judgment through champions, as the well-worn proverb says: 'May Peter bless the man to whom God gives

---

[13] *Pharsalia* 4, 593–655.
[14] *Metamorphoses* 9, 183f.
[15] *ibid.* 10, 560f.
[16] *Aeneid* V, 334f. Eurialus won because his friend Nisus obstructed his rival Salius in the race.
[17] *De officiis* 3, 10, 42. Dante is again perhaps quoting from memory, since the quotation is incomplete, omitting the reference to obstruction by hand [*aut manu depellere*] of the original.
[18] The next two chapters, which develop the notions of the race (ch. viii) and trial by combat [*duellum*] (ch. ix) in relation to the Roman empire's struggle for supremacy, are those which modern readers find most disconcerting. A spirited defence of Dante is offered by Nardi in his commentary to chapter viii and by Vinay at chapter ix.

victory', there is no doubt that the victory among those competing in the race for world domination was won in accordance
with God's judgment. The Roman people won the race to rule 2
the world against all competition. This will be clear if, when we
consider the competitors, we also consider the prize or finishing-
post. The prize or finishing-post was to rule over all mortals:
this is what we mean by 'empire'. But none achieved this except
the Roman people; they were not only the first, but indeed the
only ones to reach the finishing-post in the contest, as will appear
directly. For the first among mortals who strove to win this prize 3
was Ninus, king of the Assyrians. Although, as Orosius relates,[1]
he tried for ninety years and more with his consort Semiramis
to conquer the world by force, and subjected all of Asia to
himself, nonetheless the eastern parts of the world were never
under their rule. Ovid recalled them both in his fourth book, 4
where he says in the Pyramus episode:

> Semiramis circled the city with walls of brick;[2]

and later on:

> They were
> To meet at the tomb of Ninus and hide in the shade.[3]

The second who aspired to this prize was Vesoges, king of Egypt; 5
and although he pillaged southern and northern Asia, as Orosius
recalls,[4] yet he never conquered even half the world; for he was
turned aside from his reckless undertaking by the Scythians,
midway as it were between the starters[5] and the finishing-post.
Then Cyrus, king of the Persians, attempted the same thing. Having 6
destroyed Babylon and transferred the Babylonian empire to the
Persians, he laid down his life and along with it his ambition under
Tamiris, queen of the Scythians, without ever even reaching the
lands to the west.[6] After these Xerxes, son of Darius and king of 7
the Persians, invaded the world with such a vast number of peoples

---

[1] *Hist.* I, 4.
[2] *Metamorphoses* IV, 58.
[3] *ibid.* IV, 88.
[4] *Hist.* I, 14.
[5] i.e. the race officials who give the athletes the starting signal.
[6] *Hist.* 2, 6–7.

and with such military might that he was able to bridge the strait which separates Asia from Europe, between Sestos and Abidos. Lucan recalls this astonishing achievement in the second book of the *Pharsalia*; for he says there:

> Fame sings that proud Xerxes
> built such paths across the seas.[7]

But in the end, ignominiously driven back from what he had set
8 out to do, he was unable to win the prize. In addition to these, and after them, Alexander king of Macedon came closer than anyone else to winning the prize of monarchy. Livy relates that as he was urging the Romans to surrender through his ambassadors, he collapsed in Egypt before receiving a reply from the Romans, in the
9 middle of the race so to speak.[8] Lucan bears witness to his tomb being there in Egypt, when he says in his eighth book, inveighing against Ptolemy king of Egypt:

> Last doomed and degenerate descendant
> Of the line of Lagus, you who must surrender
> The sceptre to your own incestuous sister,
> Even though the Macedonian is preserved
> In a consecrated cave.[9]

10 'O depth of the riches both of the knowledge and wisdom of God',[10] who is not astonished at you in this connection? For you carried off Alexander from the contest when he was striving to obstruct his Roman rival in the race, so that his foolhardiness might proceed no further.
11 But that Rome won the prize in this great contest is confirmed by many testimonies. For our poet says in his first book:

> Surely you promised that from them some time,
> With passing years, the Romans were to come;

---

[7] *Pharsalia* II, 672–3; see also *Hist.* 2, 9–10.
[8] *Ab urbe condita* 9, 17f. Livy does not in fact say that Alexander died in Egypt. Orosius, *Hist.* 3, 16–20, uses the metaphor of the race à propos of Alexander's failure to fulfil his ambition ('when, as it were, he had driven his chariot around the turning post'), but says correctly that he died in Babylon. Davis (p. 103) points out, following Nardi, that only Dante speaks of failure (rather than of a transfer of power) in relation to earlier attempts at global domination.
[9] *Pharsalia* VIII, 692–4.
[10] Romans 11, 33.

> From Teucer's line restored leaders should come
> To hold the sea and all lands in their sway.[11]

And Lucan in his first book: 12

> The kingdom is divided by the sword;
> The destiny of the imperial people
> Who rule the sea and lands and the whole world
> Found no place for two men.[12]

And Boethius in his second book, when speaking of the prince of 13 the Romans, says:

> The empire that he held in sway
> From eastern sun's rise then was spread
> To where he sinks at close of day.
> Its northern march where the two Bears stand,
> Its southern bounds where the parched south wind
> Burns and bakes the arid sand.[13]

Christ's chronicler Luke, who always speaks the truth, bears witness 14 to this also, in the passage where he tells us: 'There went out a decree from Caesar Augustus, that all the world should be taxed';[14] in these words we can clearly perceive that at that time the Romans exercised jurisdiction over the whole world. From all of this it is 15 clear that the Roman people won the race against all its rivals competing for world domination; therefore they won by divine judgment, and consequently they obtained it by divine judgment; which means they obtained it by right.

ix

Furthermore whatever is acquired through trial by combat[1] is acquired by right. For wherever human judgment is unequal to the

---

[11] *Aeneid* I, 234–6.
[12] *Pharsalia* I, 109–11.
[13] *De consolatione philosophiae* 2, metr. 6, 8–13.
[14] Luke 2, 1.
[1] 'Trial by combat' seems the least unsatisfactory rendering of *duellum* in English, although it loses the etymological connection with 'two' (*duo*) to which Dante draws attention in par. 2; 'trial by champion' would be the appropriate translation if the encounter were always between individuals, but Dante uses the word to refer also to combat between two teams and two armies. The parties in conflict meet in combat having agreed that the outcome will be considered binding by both sides as representing the will of heaven. Dante goes on to explain (par. 4)

task, whether because it is wrapped in the darkness of ignorance or because no judge is available to preside, then to ensure that justice is not left abandoned we must have recourse to Him who so loved justice that, dying, he met its demands with his own blood; whence

2 the psalm: 'The Lord is just and has loved just things.'[2] Now this happens when by free agreement of both sides, not out of hatred, nor out of love, but solely out of a passionate concern for justice, we seek to know divine judgment through a clash of strength of both body and soul; we call this clash of strength trial by combat (*duellum*) because originally it was devised as combat between two

3 (*duo*) individuals. But just as in warfare all ways of reaching a resolution through negotiation must be tried first and only as a last resort do we engage in battle (and Cicero and Vegetius are in agreement in urging this, in the *De officiis*[3] and the *De re militari*[4] respectively); and just as in medical treatment everything must be tried before the knife and fire[5] and these are to be used as a last resort; in the same way care must always be taken to ensure that, when all other ways have first been investigated as a way of resolving the dispute, we have recourse to this remedy as a last resort, forced to adopt it

4 as it were by a need for justice. There are thus two identifying features of trial by combat: the first is the one we have just described; the other is the one we touched on earlier, i.e. that the contenders or champions enter the arena by mutual agreement, and not out of hatred, nor out of love, but solely out of a passionate concern for justice. And that is why Cicero spoke wisely when he touched on this subject, for what he said was: 'But wars aimed at

5 securing the crown of empire should be waged less harshly.'[6] For

that two necessary conditions must be fulfilled if it is to be a true *duellum*: it must be a solution of last resort, all other attempts to resolve the dispute having failed; and the motive of the contenders must be solely a passionate concern for justice. F. Patetta, *Le ordalie*, Torino 1890, traces the history of the *duellum* and the other types of ordeal used to ascertain God's judgment [*iudicium Dei*] from earliest times to the late Middle Ages; see also G. Neilson, *Trial by Combat*, Glasgow 1890.

[2] Psalms 10, 8 (AV 11, 7).
[3] *De officiis* 1, 11, 34.
[4] *De re militari* 3, 9.
[5] i.e. surgery and cauterization.
[6] *De officiis* 1, 12, 38. Dante appears to be citing from memory again, as the word used by Cicero is not crown [*corona*] but glory [*gloria*]. The meaning is essentially the same, but it is perhaps significant that *corona* allows Dante to make a connection with the biblical 'crown of righteousness' [*corona iustitie*] referred to in par. 19.

if these essential conditions of trial by combat have been respected – and if they have not it would not be trial by combat – is it not true that those who out of a need for justice have come to confront one another by mutual agreement through a passionate concern for justice have come to confront one another in the name of God? And if so, is not God in their midst, since he himself promises us as much in the Gospel?[7] And if God is present, is it not impious to 6 think that justice can fail to triumph – that justice which he himself so loves, as we noted above? And if justice cannot fail to triumph in trial by combat, is it not true that what is acquired through trial by combat is acquired by right? Even the pagans, before the trumpet 7 of the Gospel sounded, acknowledged the truth of this when they sought a judgment in the outcome of trial by combat. And so the 8 great Pyrrhus, who was noble by reason both of the customs of the Aeacidae[8] and of blood, gave a worthy answer when the Roman ambassadors were sent to him to ransom prisoners:

> I ask no gold, nor shall you give me payment;
> Let us decide by the sword, and not with gold,
> As warriors, not traffickers in war,
> The matter of life and death on either side.
> Let us test by our valour if Hera wants
> That you should rule or I, and what fate brings.
> Doubt not I shall restore to liberty
> Those whom fortune of war spared for their valour.
> I give them; take them.[9]

Here Pyrrhus called fortune 'Hera'; we call that same cause by the more appropriate and accurate name 'divine providence'. So let 9 champions beware that they do not make money their motive for fighting; for then it should not be called trial by combat, but a market-place of blood and justice; nor should it be thought that God is then present as arbiter, but that ancient Adversary who stirred up the quarrel. If they wish to be true champions, and not 10 traffickers in blood and justice, then as they enter the arena let them always have Pyrrhus before their eyes, Pyrrhus who when fighting

---

[7] Cf. Matthew 18, 20 (but the biblical context is very different).
[8] The Aeacidae are the descendants of Aeacus, of whom Pyrrhus claimed to be one. Aeacus was a man of great integrity, the son of Jupiter by Aegina.
[9] These lines come from Ennius, *Annales* VI, and are quoted by Cicero in *De officiis* I, 12, 38. Again there are textual differences from modern editions.

11 for supremacy disdained gold in the manner described. And if the usual objection should be urged against the truth I have shown (that opponents may be unevenly matched in strength), let the objection be refuted by the victory of David over Goliath;[10] and if the pagans want a different example, let them refute it by the victory of Hercules against Antaeus.[11] For it is very foolish to suppose that strength sustained by God in a champion might be unequal to the task.

12 By now it is sufficiently clear that what is won through trial by combat is won by right. But the Roman people acquired the empire through trial by combat; and this is confirmed by trustworthy testimony. In detailing this testimony, not only will this point become clear, but it will also be apparent that from the very beginnings of the Roman empire any matter of dispute was decided by trial by

13 combat. For at the very beginning, when a dispute arose about the abode of father Aeneas, who was the first father of the Roman people, and Turnus king of the Rutuli opposed him, in the end, in order to seek out what was God's will, the two kings agreed to fight

14 in single combat, as is related at the end of the *Aeneid*.[12] In this combat the clemency of the victor Aeneas was so great that, had he not caught sight of the belt which Turnus had taken from Pallas when he killed him, the victor would have granted life as well as

15 peace to the vanquished, as our poet's closing lines testify.[13] When two peoples had sprung up in Italy from that same Trojan root, i.e. the Romans and the Albans,[14] and a conflict had raged between them for a long time about the eagle standard and the other household gods of Troy and the honour of supremacy, in the end, by mutual agreement, in order to reach a just settlement the matter was fought out by three Horatii brothers on one side and the same number of Curiatii brothers on the other, in the presence of the kings and the peoples waiting on either side. When the three champions of the Albans and two of the Romans had been killed, the

---

[10] I Regum 17, 4–51 (AV I Samuel).

[11] See for example the account in *Pharsalia* IV, 593–653.

[12] *Aeneid* XII, 693–938. The word *duellum* is not used by Virgil, but both sides agree to abide by the outcome of the single combat between their leaders.

[13] *ibid.* XII, 938–52.

[14] Alba Longa was founded by Ascanius, the son of Aeneas. From the point of view of the Romans the household gods of the Alban families are, by descent, the 'other' household gods of Troy.

prize of victory passed to the Romans under king Hostilius. And Livy wrote a meticulous account of this episode in his first book,[15] and Orosius too confirms it.[16] Livy tells how later, respecting all the 16 rules of warfare, they fought for supremacy with the neighbouring peoples, with the Sabines and the Samnites, in the manner of a trial by combat (even though there was a vast number of combatants); and in this way of fighting with the Samnites Fortune almost repented, so to speak, of her undertaking. And Lucan reports 17 this by way of example in his second book in these words:

> What heaps of slain lay at the Colline Gate
> When the world capital and its government
> Was nearly transferred to a different seat,
> And the Samnite hoped for a heavier blow to Rome
> Than the Caudine Forks.[17]

But after the disputes between Italians had been resolved, and there 18 had as yet been no confrontation to ascertain divine judgment with the Greeks and with the Carthaginians (both of whom were striving for Empire), Fabritius fought for the Romans and Pyrrhus for the Greeks along with a vast number of soldiers for the glory of supremacy, and Rome won; and Scipio for the Italians and Hannibal for the Africans fought a war in the form of trial by combat, and the Africans were beaten by the Italians, as Livy and all Roman historians are at pains to relate.[18] Who then is now so obtuse as not 19 to see that the glorious people gained the crown of the whole world by right through trial by combat? A Roman could truly have said with the Apostle to Timothy: 'There is laid up for me a crown of righteousness';[19] 'laid up', that is, in God's eternal providence. Now 20 let the presumptuous jurists see just how far they are below that watch-tower[20] of reason from which the human mind contemplates

---

[15] *Ab urbe condita* 1, 24–6. Livy describes at length the formal agreement between the two sides that the outcome of the combat would be binding.
[16] *Hist.* 2, 4. Orosius gives no details.
[17] *Pharsalia* 2, 135–8. The Caudine Forks was a humiliating Roman defeat at the hands of the Samnites in 321 BC; the defeat of the Samnites at the Colline Gate in 82 BC was definitive.
[18] The Second Punic War is described by Livy in Books 21–30 of *Ab urbe condita*; cf. *Aeneid* VI, 842–4.
[19] 2 Timothy 4, 8.
[20] Cf. Boethius, *De consolatione philosophiae* 4, 6, who talks of the watch-tower of providence [*ex alta providentiae specula*] in just that section of the work which the

these principles, and let them be silent and be satisfied to give counsel and judgment in accordance with the sense of the law.[21]

21 And it is already clear that the Roman people acquired the empire
through trial by combat; therefore it acquired it by right; which is
our main thesis in this present book.

X

Up to this point our thesis has been proved by arguments which
are mainly based on rational principles; but now it must be proved
again from the principles of the Christian faith. For it is those who
style themselves ardent defenders of the Christian faith who most
of all have 'raged' and 'meditated vain things' against Roman authority; they have no pity for Christ's poor, who are not only
defrauded of the revenues of the churches, but whose very patrimony[1] is daily stolen; and the Church grows poor while they,

2 making a pretence of justice, shut out the dispenser of justice.[2] But
this impoverishment of the Church does not happen without God's
judgment, since her resources are not used to help the poor (whose
patrimony the Church's wealth is), and since no gratitude is shown

3 for receiving them from the empire which offers them. Let them
return where they came from: they came well, they return badly,
since they were given in good faith and badly held. What does this
matter to such shepherds? What do they care if the Church's substance is wasted, as long as the wealth of their own relatives
increases? But perhaps it is better to return to our thesis, and wait
in reverent silence for help from our Saviour.

4 I say therefore that if the Roman empire was not based on right,
Christ by his birth assented to an injustice; the consequent is false;
therefore the contradictory of the antecedent is true. For contradictory statements are mutually exclusive: if one is false, the other

---

opening of this second book calls to mind (see II, i, n. 2). Orosius, *Hist.* I, I, talks
of surveying history from a watch-tower in order to gain perspective on historical
events and take in broad patterns of significance ('viewing them as if from a
watchtower, I shall present the conflicts of the human race'): precisely what Dante
has done in Book II, and what the presumptuous jurists he here calls to account
fail to do.

[21] i.e. without presuming to judge in areas outside their competence.

[1] Cf. *Mon.* III, x, 16–17.

[2] i.e. the monarch or emperor.

must be true.[3] There is no need to demonstrate to believers that 5
the consequent is false, for if someone is a believer, he allows that
this is false; if he does not allow it, he is not a believer, and if he
is not a believer, this argument is not for him. I show the relation- 6
ship of consequentiality[4] as follows: anyone who of his own free
will complies with an edict, acknowledges by his action that the
edict is legitimate, and, since actions are more telling than words,
as Aristotle says at the end of the *Ethics*,[5] he does so more effectively
than if he gave it his verbal approval. But as his chronicler Luke
relates,[6] Christ chose to be born of his Virgin Mother under an
edict emanating from Roman authority, so that the Son of God
made man might be enrolled as a man in that unique census of the
human race; this means that he acknowledged the validity of that
edict.[7] And perhaps it is more holy to believe that the edict came 7
by divine inspiration through Caesar, so that he who had been so
long awaited in the society of men might himself be enrolled among
mortals. Therefore Christ acknowledged by his action that the edict 8
of Augustus, who embodied the authority of the Romans, was legitimate. And since someone who issues an edict legitimately must
logically have the jurisdiction to do so, it necessarily follows that

[3] Dante makes this logical point in slightly more technical language, literally 'contradictory statements can be inferred from one another by virtue of having exactly
opposite meanings' (thus by implication if one is false, the other *must* be true);
cf. *Summule*, p. 7 [*Lex contradictoriarum est quod si una est vera, reliqua est falsa,
et converso; in nulla enim materia possunt simul esse vere vel false*].

[4] i.e. show that the relationship of antecedent to consequent exists between the two
statements (If A, then B; if not B, then not A); see II, v, nn. 26 and 27. On the
'relationship of consequentiality' [*consequentia*] see *Summule*, p. 169 [*Consequentia
econtrario est quando ex opposito consequentis sequitur oppositum antecedentis. Ut* 'si
est homo est animal; ergo si est non-animal, est non-homo'; *hic enim ex opposito
consequentis, scilicet* 'non-animal', *sequitur oppositum antecedentis, scilicet* 'non-
homo'. *In contradictoriis autem non potest esse consequentia nisi econtrario*].

[5] *Ethics* 10, 1 1172a 34–5 (and cf. *Mon.* I, xiii, 4).

[6] Luke 2, 1.

[7] Orosius emphasizes the crucial significance of Christ's choice to be enrolled in
the census as a man (*Hist.* 6, 22): 'This is that earliest and most famous
acknowledgment which designated Caesar first of all men and the Romans lords
of the world; for in the census list all men were entered individually, and in it
the very Maker of all men wished to be found and enrolled as a man among
men...Neither is there any doubt that...it was by the will of our Lord Jesus
Christ that this city prospered, was protected, and brought to such heights of
power, since to her, in preference to all others, He chose to belong when He
came, thereby making it certain that He was entitled to be called a Roman citizen
according to the declaration made in the Roman census list.'

someone who acknowledges that an edict is legitimate is also acknowledging that the jurisdiction of the authority which promulgated it is legitimate; because if it were not based on right, it would

9 not be legitimate. And note that our argument, which is based on denying the consequent, although valid in its form by virtue of a common-place,[8] yet reveals its full force as a second figure syllogism, if it is then reduced to the first figure as an argument based

10 on affirming the consequent.[9] This reduction runs as follows: all injustice is assented to unjustly; Christ did not assent unjustly; therefore he did not assent to an injustice. Affirming the consequent, we get: all injustice is assented to unjustly; Christ assented to an injustice; therefore he assented unjustly.

xi

And if the Roman empire was not based on right, Adam's sin was not punished in Christ; but this is false; therefore the contradictory

2 of the proposition from which it follows is true.[1] That the consequent is false can be demonstrated as follows: since by Adam's sin we were all sinners, in the words of the Apostle 'As by one man sin entered this world, and through sin, death, so death entered into all men, in as much as all sinned';[2] if satisfaction for that sin had not been made by the death of Christ, we would still be 'the

3 children of wrath by nature',[3] that is by our corrupted nature. But

---

[8] The common-place [*locus*] referred to here is no. 31 in *Summule, Tractatus quintus, De locis*, p. 73 [*Maxima: si unum contradictorie oppositorum est verum, reliquum est falsum, et econverso*].

[9] The argument so far developed is based on the logical commonplace that contradictory statements cannot both be true (par. 4) and on the self-evident falsehood of the consequent ('Christ by his birth assented to an injustice') for any believer (pars. 4–5). Dante now offers a pair of syllogisms which reveal the 'full force' of his argument by showing that, if the consequent were to be accepted as true, then the conclusion would be not just that Christ assented to 'an injustice', but that he assented 'unjustly', i.e. a partial and limited claim would be replaced by one which is total and absolute, and therefore even more shockingly blasphemous to a believer. The text and meaning of these last two paragraphs are discussed in P. Shaw, 'Some Proposed Emendations to the Text of Dante's *Monarchia*', in *Italian Studies* 50, 1995, pp. 1–8.

[1] The form of the argument exactly parallels ii, x, 4 (see n. 3), the underlying principle again being that of a pair of contradictories, if one is true, the other must be false; see Aristotle, *De interpretatione* 6–7.

[2] Romans 5, 12.

[3] Cf. Ephesians 2, 3.

this is not the case, since the Apostle speaking of the Father in *Ephesians* says: 'He has predestined us, according to the determination of his will, to be adopted as his children through Jesus Christ unto him, to the praise and glory of his grace, with which he favoured us in his beloved son, in whom we have redemption, by his blood, remission of sins in accordance with the riches of his glory which is superabundant in us';[4] and since Christ himself, suffering punishment in his own person, says in *John*: 'It is finished';[5] for where something is finished, nothing remains to be done. As regards 4 the relationship of consequentiality, it must be borne in mind that 'punishment' is not simply 'a penalty imposed on one who does wrong', but 'a penalty imposed on the wrong-doer by one who has the legal authority to punish him'; so that if the penalty is not imposed by an authorized judge, it is not a 'punishment', but is more accurately termed a 'wrong'. Hence the man said to Moses: 'Who appointed you judge over us?'[6] Thus if Christ had not suf- 5 fered under an authorized judge, that penalty would not have been a punishment. And no judge could be authorized unless he had jurisdiction over the whole of mankind, since the whole of mankind was punished in that flesh of Christ 'who bore our sorrows', as the prophet says.[7] And Tiberius Caesar, whose representative Pilate was, would not have had jurisdiction over the whole of mankind unless the Roman empire had existed by right. This is why Herod, 6 although he did not know what he was doing (any more than Caiaphas did when he spoke the truth by heavenly decree) sent Christ back to Pilate to be judged, as Luke relates in his Gospel.[8] For Herod did not act as Tiberius' representative invested with the authority of the eagle or the authority of the senate,[9] rather he governed as the king appointed by him over a particular kingdom, and invested with the authority of the kingdom which had been entrusted to him. So let those who pass themselves off as sons of 7 the church stop attacking the Roman empire, seeing that Christ the bridegroom sanctioned it in this way at the beginning and at the

[4] Ephesians 1, 5–8.
[5] John 19, 30; cf. Matthew 27, 50. These are Christ's last words on the cross.
[6] Exodus 2, 14.
[7] Isaiah 53, 4.
[8] Luke 23, 11.
[9] i.e. he was not invested with the authority of the empire and of Rome, but only with local jurisdiction.

end of his earthly campaign.[10] And I consider it now sufficiently proven that the Roman people took over the empire of the world by right.

8   O happy people, O glorious Ausonia,[11] if only that man who weakened your empire had never been born, or at least had never been led astray by his own pious intentions.[12]

---

[10] i.e. at the beginning and end of his life.

[11] i.e. Italy.

[12] An oblique if impassioned reference to the donation of Constantine, a theme which will be developed at length in III, x (see n. 1). There is a clear parallel with the close of Book I: just as that book in its final chapter had spoken of Christ's birth, so now Book II in its final chapter speaks of Christ's death – the key events in human history which legitimize the Roman empire. There may be a deliberate echo here of Christ's words about Judas at the last supper, as reported in Matthew 26, 24 [*Bonum erat ei si natus non fuisset homo ille*, 'It would have been better for that man not to have been born'].

Book Three

i

'He shut the lions' mouths, and they did not harm me, for in his sight righteousness was found in me.'[1]

At the beginning of this work it was proposed to inquire into three questions, within the limits allowed by the subject-matter; the first two of them have been dealt with sufficiently, I believe, in the previous books. Now it remains to deal with the third, the truth of 2 which cannot be brought to light without putting certain people to shame, and will therefore perhaps be a cause of some resentment against me. But since truth from its unchangeable throne implores 3 us, and Solomon too, entering the forest of *Proverbs*,[2] teaches us by his own example to meditate on truth and loathe wickedness; and since our authority on morals, Aristotle, urges us to destroy what touches us closely for the sake of maintaining truth;[3] then having taken heart from the words of Daniel cited above, in which divine power is said to be a shield of the defenders of truth, and putting on 'the breast-plate of faith' as Paul exhorts us,[4] afire with that burning coal which one of the seraphim took from the heavenly altar to touch Isaiah's lips,[5] I shall enter the present arena, and, by his arm who freed us from the power of darkness[6] with his blood,

[1] Daniel 6, 22.
[2] Proverbs 8, 7.
[3] *Ethics* 1, 6 1096a 13–15.
[4] 1 Thessalonians 5, 8.
[5] Isaiah 6, 6–7.
[6] Cf. Colossians 1, 13.

before the eyes of the world I shall cast out the wicked and the
4 lying from the ring. What should I fear, when the Spirit who is
coeternal with the Father and the Son says through the mouth of
David: 'the righteous shall be in everlasting remembrance and shall
not be afraid of ill report'.[7]

5   The present question, therefore, which we are now to investigate,
concerns the 'two great lights',[8] that is the Roman Pope and the
Roman Prince; and the point at issue is whether the authority of
the Roman monarch, who is monarch of the world by right, as was
proved in the second book, derives directly from God or else from
some vicar or minister of God, by which I mean Peter's successor,
who assuredly holds the keys to the kingdom of heaven.

ii

In order to investigate this question, some principle must be
adopted (just as it was with the previous ones[1]) on whose validity
the arguments designed to reveal the truth can be based; for without
an agreed principle what point is there in striving, even though one
speaks the truth, since only such a principle provides a basis for
2 the middle terms to be adopted? So let this inviolable truth be
formulated at the outset: what is contrary to nature's intention is
against God's will. For if this were not true, its contradictory would
not be false, i.e. what is contrary to nature's intention is not against
3 God's will. And if this is not false, nor are those things which
follow from it;[2] for it is impossible in necessary consequences for
4 the consequent to be false without the antecedent being false.[3] But

---

[7] Psalms 111, 7 (AV 112, 6–7). The phrase *ab auditione mala* is translated in the
AV and the *New Revised Standard Version* '(afraid) of evil tidings', but Dante
clearly understands the phrase to mean being spoken ill of by others.

[8] Genesis 1, 16.

[1] Cf. I, ii and II, ii: the three books are exactly parallel in structure.

[2] Having stated his principle (par. 2), Dante demonstrates its truth (by default, as
it were) by showing that patently absurd consequences would follow if its opposite
were true. This is known as a proof *per impossibile*, see Aristotle, *Prior Analytics*
I, 23 41a 21–5; 2, 11–14. The underlying assumption is again that of two strict
opposites, if one is true, the other must be false: teasing out the consequences of
the *contradictorium* occupies the rest of the chapter, whose concluding sentence
summarizes the procedure.

[3] The relationship between antecedent and consequent is a *necessary* one: if man,
then (necessarily, by definition) animal; hence if not animal, then (of necessity)
not man, see II, v, notes 26 and 27.

one of two things must necessarily follow if a thing is not against one's will: one must either will it or not will it; just as, if one does not hate something, it necessarily follows that one either loves it or does not love it; for not loving is not the same as hating, and the fact that one does not will something is not the same as its being against one's will, as is self-evident. If these conclusions are not false, this will not be false either: 'God wills what he does not will'; and nothing could be more false than this. I prove the truth of this 5 affirmation[4] as follows: it is obvious that God wills the goal of nature, otherwise he would move the heavens to no purpose – not a tenable proposition. If God willed the obstructing of nature's goal, he would also will the goal of that obstructing, for otherwise he would once again will to no effect; and since the aim of an obstruction is to prevent what is obstructed from happening, it would follow that God willed that nature should not fulfil its goal – which he is said to will. But if God did not will the obstructing of nature's 6 goal, inasmuch as he did not will it, it would follow logically from his not willing that he was indifferent to whether the obstructing took place or did not take place; but one who is indifferent to an obstruction is indifferent to the thing which can be obstructed, and therefore does not have it in his will; and what someone does not have in his will, he does not will. Therefore if the goal of nature 7 can be obstructed – which it can – it necessarily follows that God does not will the goal of nature; and thus our earlier conclusion follows, namely that God wills what he does not will. That principle from whose contradictory such absurd consequences follow is therefore unquestionably true.

iii

By way of preamble it should be noted that the truth of the first question needed to be demonstrated more in order to eliminate ignorance than to resolve a dispute; but the truth of the second question addressed ignorance and dispute in almost equal measure, for there are many things we do not know about which we do not

---

[4] i.e. of the claim that the obviously absurd statement 'God wills what he does not will' [*Deus vult quod non vult*] follows from the unobjectionable logical point that if something is not against one's will, one either wills it or is indifferent to it (i.e. that *non nolle* implies either *velle* (par. 5) or *non velle* (par. 6–7)).

2 argue. The geometrician, for example, does not know how to square the circle,[1] but he does not argue about it; the theologian for his part does not know how many angels there are, yet he does not engage in dispute about the matter; the Egyptian likewise is ignorant of the civilization of the Scythians,[2] yet he does not on this account

3 argue about their civilization. But the truth concerning this third question is so fiercely disputed that, just as in other matters it is ignorance which gives rise to dispute, so here it is rather the dispute

4 which is the cause of ignorance. For it often happens that men who guide their will by the light of reason, should they be swayed by misguided impulses, put the light of reason behind them and are dragged by passion like blind men, and yet obstinately deny their

5 own blindness. And so it happens very often that not only does falsehood find defenders, but that many stray beyond their own borders and make incursions into the territory of others, where, understanding nothing, they quite fail to make themselves understood; and thus they provoke some people to anger, others to dis-

6 dain, and many to mirth. Now three classes of people in particular

7 fiercely oppose the truth we are investigating. For the supreme Pontiff, the vicar of our Lord Jesus Christ and Peter's successor, to whom we owe not what is due to Christ but what is due to Peter,[3] perhaps motivated by a zealous concern for the keys, and with him other shepherds of the Christian flock and others who I believe act only out of zealous concern for Mother Church: these people oppose the truth I am about to demonstrate – perhaps, as I said,

8 out of zealous concern and not out of pride. Certain others, however, whose stubborn greed has extinguished the light of reason, and who, having the devil as their father,[4] yet profess themselves to be sons of the church, not only stir up quarrels in relation to this question, but, loathing the very expression 'most sacred sovereign authority', would even impudently deny the first principles which

---
[1] The example of squaring the circle is used repeatedly by Aristotle, e.g. *Sophistical Refutations* 11, 171b 15, 172a 2f.; *Physics* 1, 185a 14–17.
[2] Cf. *Ethics* 3, 3 1112a 28–30.
[3] The distinction between what is due to Christ and what to Peter will prove to be a fundamental principle underlying the argument of Book III.
[4] Cf. John 8, 44. This second category of opponents probably consists of princes and kings hostile to the emperor.

66

underlie this question and those previously discussed.[5] There is also 9
a third category, called decretalists[6] – ignorant and lacking in any
philosophical or theological training – who argue their case exclusively with reference to their decretals[7] (which I certainly think
worthy of veneration); trusting in their authoritativeness, I believe,
they disparage the empire. Nor is this a cause for astonishment, 10
since I once heard one of them[8] say and stubbornly insist that the
traditions of the church are the foundation of faith. Let this wicked
belief be removed from the minds of mortals by those who, before
the traditions of the church, believed in Christ the Son of God
(whether Christ to come or Christ present or Christ already
crucified), and who in believing hoped, and hoping burned with
love, and burning with love became co-heirs along with him,[9] as
the world does not doubt. And in order that such people should 11
be entirely excluded from the present arena, it must be borne in
mind that some scriptures preceded the church, others coincided
with the founding of the church, and others followed it. Before the 12
church are the Old and New Testaments, which 'he hath com-
manded for ever', as the Prophet says;[10] for this is what the church
says speaking to her bridegroom: 'Draw me after thee.'[11] Contem- 13
poraneous with the church are those venerated principal councils[12]
at which Christ was present, as no believer doubts, since we know
that he said to the disciples as he was about to ascend to heaven:

---

[5] Dante elsewhere cites Aristotle to the effect that there is no point in arguing with
those who deny first principles.
[6] i.e. commentators on the decretals, see n. 7.
[7] The decretals are 'the papal decrees or epistles, usually written in reply to some
question of general ecclesiastical law; they form the groundwork of a large part
of the law of the Church. A compilation of them, with additions of his own, was
issued by Pope Gregory IX in 1234, and with further additions, by Pope Boniface
VIII in 1298, and again, in 1314, by Pope Clement V. Previously, some time
before 1150, Gratian of Bologna had published his Decretum, a general collection
of canons, papal epistles, and sentences of fathers, in imitation of the Pandects;
this work appears to have been the chief authority on the canon law in the Middle
Ages' (*Dict.* p. 220).
[8] Attempts to identify the individual in question have proved fruitless.
[9] Cf. Romans 8, 17.
[10] Psalms 110, 9 (AV 111, 9).
[11] Song of Solomon 1, 3. The bridegroom is Christ.
[12] The first four ecumenical councils, i.e. the Councils of Nicaea (325), Constantinople (381), Ephesus (431) and Chalcedon (451).

'Lo, I am with you always, even unto the end of the world', as Matthew bears witness.[13] There are also the writings of the doctors of the church, of Augustine and others; anyone who doubts that they were helped by the Holy Spirit has either entirely failed to

14 see their fruits or, if he has seen them, has not tasted them. Then after the church come the traditions called 'decretals', which, while certainly to be revered on account of their apostolic authority, must yet take second place to the fundamental scriptures, given that

15 Christ reproached the priests for doing the opposite. For when they asked: 'Why do thy disciples transgress the tradition of the elders?' – for they did not wash their hands – Christ answered them (Matthew is our witness): 'Why do ye also transgress the commandment of God by your tradition?'[14] By this he gave to understand

16 clearly enough that tradition takes second place. Now if the traditions of the church come after the church, as has been shown, it must be the case that the church does not derive its authority from the traditions, but that the traditions derive their authority from the church. And so those who rely only on traditions must be excluded from the arena, as we said; for those who seek to grasp this truth must conduct their investigation by starting from those

17 things from which the church's authority comes. And so, having excluded these people, others must also be excluded who, covered with crows' feathers, make a show of being white sheep in the Lord's flock. Such people are the sons of wickedness who, in order to carry out their shameful designs, prostitute their mother, drive out their brothers, and finally refuse to have a judge. Why should we seek to convince them, since, slaves to their own greed, they would be incapable of seeing first principles?

18 It therefore remains to argue the case only with those who, motivated by some zealous concern for Mother Church, are unaware of that truth which we seek; and so it is with them – showing that reverence which a dutiful son owes his father, a dutiful son owes his mother, devout towards Christ, devout towards the Church, devout towards the shepherd, and devout towards all who profess the Christian religion – that I engage in battle in this book in the cause of truth.[15]

---

[13] Matthew 28, 20.
[14] Matthew 15, 1–3.
[15] The phrase echoes *Ethics* 1, 6 1096a 14–15.

iv

The whole of the argument which follows will therefore be addressed to those people who assert that the authority of the empire is dependent on the authority of the church in the same way as a builder is dependent on the architect.[1] They are influenced by a number of different arguments, which they draw from the holy Scriptures and from certain actions both of the supreme Pontiff and the emperor himself; but they seek to have some support from reason on their side as well.[2] Firstly they 2 say, basing themselves on *Genesis*,[3] that God created 'two great lights' – a greater light and a lesser light – so that one might rule the day and the other rule the night; these they took in an allegorical sense to mean the two powers, i.e. the spiritual and the temporal. They then go on to argue that, just as the moon, 3 which is the lesser light, has no light except that which it receives from the sun, in the same way the temporal power has no authority except that which it receives from the spiritual power. In order to refute this and other arguments of theirs, it must 4 first be borne in mind that, as Aristotle states in the *Sophistical Refutations*,[4] to refute an argument is to expose an error. And since an error may occur in the content and in the form of an argument, there are two ways in which an argument can be flawed: either because a false premiss has been adopted, or because the logic is faulty; both of these charges were made against Parmenides and Melissus by Aristotle when he said: 'They adopt false premisses and use invalid syllogisms.'[5] And here I am taking 'false' in a broad sense to include the unlikely, which is the equivalent of falsehood when the question is one of

---

[1] Cf. Aristotle, *Metaphysics* I, 1 where the hierarchical distinction, which was to become a medieval commonplace, reflects the difference between a theoretical and a practical grasp of a discipline.

[2] The arguments of Dante's opponents drawn from the Scriptures will occupy chs. iv–ix; those based on the historical actions of pope and emperor chs. x–xi; and the argument from reason ch. xii. Chs. xiii–xvi will develop Dante's arguments in support of his own thesis.

[3] Genesis I, 16. The allegorical interpretation of this passage dates from as early as the fourth century; see M. Maccarrone, 'Il terzo libro della *Monarchia*', in *Studi danteschi* 33, 1955, p. 33.

[4] *Sophistical Refutations* 18, 176b 29.

[5] *Physics* I, 3 186a 6f.

5 likelihood.[6] If the error is a formal one, the conclusion has to be demolished by the person who wishes to refute it, by showing that it does not observe the rules of syllogistic argument. If on the other hand the error is one of content, it is because one of the premisses adopted is either false without qualification or else false in a certain respect. If it is false without qualification, then the argument is refuted by demolishing the premiss; if it is false in a certain respect, then it is refuted by drawing distinctions.

6 Once this has been grasped, then to reach a better understanding of the refutation of this point and those which follow, it must be borne in mind that one can make two kinds of error when dealing with the mystical sense: either looking for it where it does not exist,

7 or taking it in some inadmissible way. À propos of the first of these Augustine says in the *De civitate Dei* : 'It must not be thought that every reported event has a further meaning; but those which have no further meaning are also included for the sake of those which do have such a meaning. Only the ploughshare breaks up the soil, but for this to happen the other parts of the plough are necessary as

8 well.'[7] As regards the second the same writer says in the *De doctrina christiana*, speaking of detecting some other meaning in the scriptures than the man who wrote them, that 'it is the same mistake as if one were to abandon the highway and yet proceed by a round-about route to the same place the highway leads to'; and he adds: 'It must be pointed out that the habit of going off the highway may

9 force one to take cross-roads and wrong roads.'[8] And he goes on to indicate why this is to be avoided when dealing with the Scriptures, saying: 'Faith will waver if the authority of the Holy Scriptures is

10 shaken.' I therefore say that if such things are done out of ignorance, the mistake should be carefully pointed out and then excused, just as one would excuse someone who feared a lion in the clouds; but if such things are done deliberately, those who make this mistake should be treated no differently from tyrants who do not observe public rights for the common welfare, but seek to turn them to their

---

[6] On likelihood or probability, see Aristotle, *Topics* 1,1: in matters where it is impossible to have certainty we deal with reputable opinion, plausible propositions; and see *Summule* vii, 16.

[7] *De civitate Dei* 16, 2.

[8] *De doctrina christiana* 1, 36–7. It is interesting that only in this chapter is Augustine quoted, and then on a point of methodology, not of historical fact or interpretation.

own advantage. O supreme wickedness, even if it should happen in 11
dreams, to abuse the intention of the eternal Spirit! For this is not
a sin against Moses, nor against David, nor Job, nor Matthew, nor
Paul, but against the Holy Spirit who speaks through them.[9] For
although there are many who record the divine word, it is God
alone who dictates, deigning to reveal his pleasure to us through
the pens of many men.

Having made these preliminary observations, with reference to 12
the point made earlier I now proceed to refute that claim of theirs
that those two lights allegorically signify these two kinds of power.
The whole force of their argument lies in this claim. That this 13
interpretation is completely untenable can be demonstrated in two
ways. Firstly, given that these two kinds of power are accidental
properties[10] of man, God would seem to have perverted the natural
order by producing accidents before their subject, which is an
absurd claim to make about God; for those two lights were created
on the fourth day and man on the sixth, as is clear from the Bible.[11]
Further, given that those two powers guide men towards certain 14
ends, as we shall see presently, if man had remained in the state of
innocence in which he was created by God, he would have had no
need of such guidance; such powers are thus remedies for the
infirmity of sin.[12] Therefore since on the fourth day man was not 15
only not a sinner but he did not even exist, it would have been
pointless to produce remedies; and this is against divine goodness.
For it would be a foolish doctor who, before a man's birth, prepared
a poultice for a future abscess. It therefore cannot be maintained 16
that on the fourth day God created these two powers; and consequently Moses' meaning cannot have been what they pretend. This 17
argument can also be refuted, if we tolerate the false premiss, by
making a distinction; for a refutation based on a distinction is kinder
to one's adversary, in that he does not appear to be asserting an
outright falsehood, as a refutation based on demolishing his premiss

---

[9] Cf. 2 Peter 1, 21.
[10] On the fundamental Aristotelian distinction between accident and substance, see
Categories 7.
[11] Genesis 1, 19 and 31.
[12] It is a matter of debate whether there is an unexamined conflict between the view
here expressed of the state as a 'remedy for sin' [*remedium peccati*] (i.e. a direct
consequence of Adam's sin), and the view expressed in Book I of the state as a
natural political organization reflecting man's essential nature.

makes him appear to do. I therefore say that although the moon does not have light in abundance except in so far as it receives it from the sun, it does not follow from this that the moon derives

18 from the sun. For it must be grasped that the moon's existence is one thing, its power another, and its function another again. As far as its existence is concerned, the moon is in no way dependent on the sun; nor is it as far as its powers are concerned, nor in an absolute sense as far as its function is concerned; for its movement occurs by its own motion, and its influence comes from its own

19 rays; it has some light of its own, as is apparent in its eclipse.[13] But as far as functioning better and more efficaciously is concerned, it receives something from the sun, namely abundant light; having

20 received this, it operates more efficaciously. Thus I say that the temporal realm does not owe its existence to the spiritual realm, nor its power (which is its authority), and not even its function in an absolute sense; but it does receive from it the capacity to operate more efficaciously through the light of grace which in heaven and

21 on earth the blessing of the supreme Pontiff infuses into it. And thus the argument contained a formal error, for the predicate in the conclusion was not the same as the predicate of the major premiss, as is obvious; for it runs like this: the moon receives its light from the sun, which is the spiritual power; the temporal power is the moon; therefore the temporal power receives its authority from the

22 spiritual power. For in the predicate of the major premiss they put 'light', whereas in the predicate of the conclusion they put 'authority', and these are two different things in respect of their subject and their meaning, as we have seen.[14]

V

They also take an argument from the text of Moses,[1] saying that from the loins of Jacob there came forth a prefiguration of these two powers, in the persons of Levi and Judah: the one was the father of the priesthood, the other of temporal power. From this

---

[13] That the faint light observable during a lunar eclipse is an effect caused by the reflection of solar rays only became apparent with Galileo.

[14] It is a basic principle that a syllogism uses only three terms; see *Mon.* III, vii, 3 (and n. 2).

[1] Genesis 29, 34–5.

they go on to argue: the church stands in the same relation to the empire as Levi stood to Judah; Levi preceded Judah in his birth, as we read in the biblical account; therefore the church precedes the empire in authority. Now this point too is easily refuted, for 2 when they say that Levi and Judah, the sons of Jacob, prefigure those powers, I could refute it in the same way by denying the premiss; but let us concede it. And when by their reasoning they 3 reach the conclusion 'as Levi preceded in birth so the church precedes in authority', I say again that the predicate of the conclusion is a different thing from the predicate of the major premiss; for 'authority' is one thing and 'birth' another, both in respect of their subject and their meaning; and thus there is a logical flaw in the argument. And the reasoning goes like this: A precedes B in C; D is to E as A is to B; therefore D precedes E in F; but F and C are different things. And if they object saying that F follows from C, 4 that is authority follows from seniority by birth, and that the consequent can rightly be set in the place of the antecedent,[2] as 'animal' can be set in the place of 'man', I say that this is false: for there are many people who have seniority by birth who not only do not rank higher in authority, but are in fact outranked by people younger than themselves; as is clearly the case where bishops are younger than their archdeacons. And thus their objection is seen 5 to be marred by the fallacy of 'treating what is not a cause as a cause'.[3]

vi

Then from the text of the first book of *Kings*[1] they take the creation and deposition of Saul, and they say that King Saul was placed on the throne and removed from it by Samuel, who was acting as God's vicar by his command, as we read in the biblical account. And from 2 this they argue that just as he, as God's vicar, had the authority to give and take away temporal power and transfer it to someone else, so now too God's vicar, the head of the universal church, has the authority to give and to take away and even to transfer the sceptre

[2] See *Mon.* II, v, n. 27.
[3] On the 'fallacy of the false cause' see Aristotle, *Sophistical Refutations* 5, 167b 20f. and 6, 168b 22f.; and *Summule* VII, 164–70.
[1] 1 Regum 10, 1 and 15, 23–8; 16, 13 (AV 1 Samuel).

of temporal power; from which it would undoubtedly follow that

3 imperial authority would be dependent in the way they claim. This argument too must be answered by denying their claim that Samuel was God's vicar, because he acted on that occasion not as vicar but as a special emissary for a particular purpose, that is to say as a messenger bearing God's express command: this is clear because

4 he did and reported only what God told him to. For it must be borne in mind that it is one thing to be a vicar, and quite another to be a messenger or minister; just as it is one thing to be a writer

5 and another to be an interpreter.[2] For a vicar is a person to whom jurisdiction is entrusted within the terms of the law or at his own discretion; and thus within the limits of the jurisdiction entrusted to him he can take action by applying the law or using his own discretion in matters of which his lord knows nothing. But a messenger *qua* messenger cannot do this; for just as a hammer functions only by virtue of the craftsman using it, so a messenger too is

6 entirely dependent on the will of the person who sends him. It does not follow, then, that if God did that using Samuel as his messenger, the vicar of God may do it. For God has done, does and will do many things through his angels which the vicar of God, Peter's

7 successor, could not do. Hence their argument is 'from the whole to the part', in affirmative form like this: 'man can see and hear; therefore the eye can see and hear'. And this is not valid; it would be valid if put into negative form like this: 'man cannot fly; therefore man's arms cannot fly'. And in the same way we would have: 'God cannot through a messenger make undone things that have once been done, as Agathon observed:[3] therefore his vicar cannot do so either'.

vii

They also take the offerings of the Magi from the text of *Matthew*,[1] saying that Christ received the frankincense along with the gold to signify that he was lord and ruler of spiritual and temporal things;

---

[2] The difference is one of independence or relative autonomy, the interpreter being tied to and limited by the text he interprets.

[3] *Ethics* 6, 2 1139b 8–11. The original is talking about God himself; Dante adds the words 'through a messenger' [*per nuntium*].

[1] Matthew 2, 1–13.

from this they infer that Christ's vicar is the lord and ruler of the
same things, and thus has authority over both of them. In reply to 2
this, I accept the literal meaning of Matthew and their interpretation of it, but I reject what they try to infer from it. Their syllogism
runs like this: 'God is the Lord of spiritual and temporal things;
the supreme Pontiff is God's vicar; therefore he is the lord of spiritual and temporal things'. For each of the premisses is true, but 3
the middle term is not the same and the argument uses four terms,
so that the syllogism contains a formal error, as is clear from what
is said in the *Prior Analytics*.[2] For 'God', the subject in the major
premiss, is one thing, and 'God's vicar', the predicate in the minor
premiss, is a different thing. And if anyone were to base an objec- 4
tion on a vicar's being equivalent, the objection has no force, for
no vicariate, human or divine, can be equivalent to the primary
authority; and this is easy to see. For we know that Peter's successor 5
is not the equivalent of divine authority at least as regards the
workings of nature, for he could not make earth rise nor fire descend
by virtue of the office entrusted to him. Nor could all things be 6
entrusted to him by God, since God certainly could not entrust to
him the power to create and the power to baptize,[3] as is quite apparent, although Peter Lombard expressed the contrary opinion in his
fourth book.[4] We also know that a man's vicar, in as much as he 7
is his vicar, is not equivalent to him, because no one can give away
what does not belong to him. A prince's authority belongs to a
prince only as something for his use, for no prince can confer authority on himself; he can accept it and renounce it, but he cannot
create another prince, for the creation of a prince is not dependent
on a prince. If this is the case, it is clear that no prince can appoint 8
a vicar to take his place who is equivalent to him in all things; thus
the objection has no force.

viii

They likewise take from the text of *Matthew* those words of Christ
to Peter: 'And whatsoever thou shalt bind on earth shall be bound

---

[2] *Prior Analytics* 1, 25 41b 36f.
[3] i.e. the power to validate baptism; on the theological point that the pope acts only
as God's minister when he baptizes, see Nardi's essay 'Dal *Convivio* alla *Commedia*', in the book of the same title, Roma 1960, pp. 109–12.
[4] *Sententiae* 4, 5.

in heaven; and whatsoever thou shalt loose on earth shall be loosed in heaven.'[1] This was also said to all the apostles (they take the

2 same thing from the text both of *Matthew* and of *John*). On this they base their argument that God has granted to Peter's successor the power to bind and loose all things; and they infer from this that he can 'loose' the laws and decrees of the empire, and 'bind' laws and decrees in the place of the temporal power; and what

3 they claim would indeed logically follow. This argument must be answered by drawing a distinction in relation to the major premiss of the syllogism they use. Their syllogism takes this form: 'Peter could loose and bind all things; Peter's successor can do anything Peter could do; therefore Peter's successor can loose and bind all things'. From this they deduce that he can loose and bind the auth-

4 ority and the decrees of the empire.[2] I grant the minor premiss, but I do not grant the major premiss without drawing a distinction. And thus I say that this universal sign 'all', which is contained in 'whatsoever', never refers beyond the scope of the term to which

5 it refers. For example if I say 'all animals run', the word 'all' refers to every creature which is included within the class 'animal'; but if I say 'all men run', then here the universal sign refers only to those beings that come into the category 'man'; and when I say 'all grammarians', then the range of reference is even narrower.

6 For this reason one must always take into consideration what it is that the universal sign refers to; having done so, and having established the nature and the scope of the term to which it refers, the

7 range of its reference will be readily apparent.[3] So when the statement is made 'whatsoever thou shalt bind', if the word 'whatsoever' were taken in an absolute sense, what they say would be true; and Peter could not only do that, but also loose a wife from her husband and bind her to another while the first was still alive; and this he certainly cannot do. He could also absolve me without my having

---

[1] Matthew 16, 19.

[2] This argument, one of those most frequently advanced by the hierocrats, had been used in *Unam sanctam*, Boniface VIII's Bull of 18 November 1302. A full account of the history of its use is given in J. A. Watt, 'The Theory of Papal Monarchy in the Thirteenth Century. The Contribution of the Canonists', in *Traditio* 20, 1964, pp. 179–317.

[3] On the logical principle Dante is here invoking, see *Summule XII, De distributionibus*.

repented, which even God himself could not do.[4] This being so 8
then, it is clear that the range of reference is to be taken not in an
absolute sense, but in relation to something. That it is to be taken
in relation to something is clear enough when we consider what
was granted to him, for it is precisely to this that the range of
reference is linked. For Christ says to Peter: 'I will give unto thee 9
the keys of the kingdom of heaven', that is: 'I shall make you gate-
keeper of the kingdom of heaven.' He then adds 'and whatsoever',
which is to say 'all that', i.e. 'and all that pertains to this office thou
shalt have the power to loose and bind'. And thus the universal 10
sign which is contained in 'whatsoever' is limited in its reference
by the office of the keys of the kingdom of heaven; and if it is taken
in this way, the proposition is true; but it is not true in an absolute
sense, as is clear. And thus I say that, although Peter's successor 11
can loose and bind as the office entrusted to Peter requires, nonetheless it does not follow from this that he can loose or bind the
decrees or the laws of the empire, as they maintained, unless they
were further to prove that this pertained to the office of the keys.
That the opposite is the case will be demonstrated below.[5]

ix

They also take those words spoken by Peter to Christ in *Luke*, when
he says: 'Behold, here are two swords';[1] and they maintain that by
those two swords we are to understand the two powers mentioned
earlier, which Peter said were present wherever he was (i.e.
belonged to him); and from this they argue that those two powers
as far as their authority is concerned reside with Peter's successor.
This too must be answered by demolishing the allegorical interpret- 2
ation on which they base their argument. For they claim that those
two swords alluded to by Peter signify the two powers mentioned.
This must be utterly rejected, both because that reply would have
been at odds with Christ's intention, and because Peter as was his

---

[4] These are classic instances of the absurd consequences of an absolutist interpretation of papal powers. On the prohibition of divorce, see Matthew 19, 9; Mark
10, 11–12; Luke 16, 18.
[5] In ch. xiv.
[1] Luke 22, 38. The words were in fact spoken not by Peter but by all the apostles.

habit answered unreflectingly, only considering the surface of
3 things.[2] It will not be hard to see that the reply was at odds with
Christ's intention, if we take into consideration the words which
precede it and the occasion which gave rise to them. Thus it must
be borne in mind that this was said on the day of the Last Supper;
hence Luke begins his account earlier: 'Then came the day of
unleavened bread, when the Paschal lamb must be killed';[3] it was
during this supper that Christ foretold his impending passion, in
4 which he must be separated from his disciples. It must likewise be
borne in mind that when those words were uttered all twelve disciples were present; hence shortly after the words cited Luke says:
'And when the hour was come, he sat down, and the twelve apostles
5 with him.'[4] From here the conversation continued until he came to
this: 'When I sent you forth without purse, and scrip, and shoes,
lacked ye any thing? And they said, Nothing. Then said he unto
them, But now, he that hath a purse, let him take it, and likewise
his scrip; and he that hath no sword, let him sell his garment, and
6 buy one.'[5] From this Christ's meaning is clear enough; for he did
not say: 'Buy or obtain two swords', but twelve, since he said to
the twelve apostles 'he that hath no sword, let him buy one', so
7 that each of them might have one. Furthermore he said this as he
was warning them of the persecution and contempt they would face,
as though to say: 'As long as I was with you, you were accepted;
now you will be driven out; so that you must acquire for yourselves
even those things which once I forbade you to have, for you will
8 need them'. And thus if Peter's reply, which is in response to this,
did have the meaning they claim, it would still have been at odds
with what Christ intended; and Christ would have reproached him
for this, as he did reproach him many times, when he replied not
knowing what he was saying. On this occasion he did not do so,
but let it pass, saying to him: 'That is enough'; as though to say:
'I say this because of your need; but if each of you cannot have
9 one, two will suffice.' And that Peter was in the habit of speaking
without reflecting is proved by his hasty and unthinking impul-

---

[2] Dante refutes the allegorical interpretation of his opponents with these two arguments, which will be elaborated respectively in pars. 3–8 and 9–17.
[3] Luke 22, 7.
[4] Luke 22, 14.
[5] Luke 22, 35–6.

siveness, which came not just from the sincerity of his faith, but, I think, from his simple and ingenuous nature. All Christ's evangelists testify to this impulsiveness of his. For Matthew writes that 10 when Jesus asked his disciples: 'Who do you say that I am?', Peter replied before all the others: 'You are Christ, the son of the living God.'[6] He also writes that when Christ said to the disciples that he must go to Jerusalem and suffer many things, Peter took him aside and began to rebuke him, saying: 'Be it far from thee, Lord; this shall not be unto you'; and Christ, turning to him, reproached him, saying: 'Get thee behind me, Satan.'[7] He also writes that on the 11 Mount of the Transfiguration, in the presence of Christ, Moses and Elias and the two sons of Zebedee, Peter said: 'Lord, it is good for us to be here; if thou wilt, let us make here three tabernacles; one for thee, and one for Moses, and one for Elias.'[8] Likewise he writes 12 that when the disciples were in their boat at night and Christ walked on the water, Peter said: 'Lord, if it be thou, bid me come unto thee on the water.'[9] Again he writes that, when Christ foretold to 13 his disciples their desertion of him, Peter replied: 'Though all men shall become deserters because of thee, yet will I never desert thee';[10] and later: 'Though I should die with thee, yet I will not deny thee.'[11] And Mark too bears witness to this;[12] Luke for his 14 part writes that Peter also said to Christ, just before the words quoted above about the swords: 'Lord, I am ready to go with thee, both into prison and to death.'[13] And John says of him that when 15 Christ wished to wash his feet, Peter said to him: 'Lord, dost thou wash my feet?'; and later: 'Thou shalt never wash my feet.'[14] He 16 also says that he struck the servant of the high priest with his sword,[15] and all four of them relate this.[16] John also says that when

---

[6] Matthew 16, 15–16.
[7] Matthew 16, 21–3.
[8] Matthew 17, 3–4.
[9] Matthew 14, 28.
[10] The AV translates: Though all men shall be offended because of thee, yet will I never be offended.
[11] Matthew 26, 31–5.
[12] Mark 14, 29–31.
[13] Luke 22, 33–4.
[14] John 13, 6–8.
[15] John 18, 10.
[16] Matthew 26, 51–2; Mark 14, 47; Luke 22, 50–2. These three accounts do not name Peter.

Peter came to the tomb he went straight in, seeing the other disciple hesitating at the entrance.[17] Again he says that, when Jesus was on the sea shore after the Resurrection, 'when Peter heard that it was the Lord, he girt his fisher's coat unto him (for he was naked), and did cast himself into the sea'.[18] Finally he says that when Peter saw

17 John, he said to Jesus: 'Lord, and what shall this man do?'[19] It is helpful to have listed these episodes involving our Archimandrite in praise of his ingenuousness, for they show quite clearly that when he spoke of the two swords he was answering Christ with no deeper

18 meaning in mind. For if those words of Christ and Peter are to be understood figuratively, they are not to be made to bear the meaning those people claim, but they are to be related to the meaning of that sword of which Matthew writes in this way: 'Think not that I am come to send peace on earth: I came not to send peace, but a sword. For I am come to set a man at variance against his father,'

19 etc.[20] This happens both with words and with actions; that is why Luke spoke to Theophilus of the things 'that Jesus began both to do and teach'.[21] This is the sword Christ instructed them to obtain, and to which Peter was referring when he answered that there were two of them there. For they were ready both for the words and for the actions by means of which they would bring about what Christ said he had come to do by the sword, as has been said.

X

Again, some people maintain that the Emperor Constantine, cured of leprosy by the intercession of Sylvester who was then supreme Pontiff, made a gift to the church of the seat of empire (i.e. Rome),

2 along with many other imperial privileges.[1] From this they argue

---

[17] John 20, 4–6.

[18] John 21, 7.

[19] John 22, 21.

[20] Matthew 10, 34–5. Dante now suggests an alternative allegorical interpretation of the swords.

[21] Acts 1, 1. Commentators have not identified a source for this interpretation of Luke's words, which appears to be Dante's own.

[1] This supposed gift to the church, known as the 'donation of Constantine', was in Dante's eyes the key event in human history which explained the sorry state of the modern world, see *Mon.* I, xvi, 3 and II, xi, 8. By giving 'Rome and all the provinces, districts and cities of Italy and the West' to Pope Sylvester, Constantine broke up what should have been an indissoluble unity, and set the church

that since that time no one can take on those imperial privileges unless he receives them from the church, to whom (they say) they belong; and it would indeed follow from this that the one authority was dependent on the other, as they claim.

Having stated and refuted those arguments which appeared to 3 be based on the word of God, it now remains to state and refute those which are based on human actions and human reason. The first of these is the one just referred to, which they formulate as a syllogism in this way: 'those things which belong to the church can only be held legitimately by someone to whom the church has granted them' (and this we concede); 'Roman sovereign authority belongs to the church; therefore no one can hold it legitimately unless granted it by the church'; and they prove the minor premiss with reference to what was touched on earlier about Constantine. It is this minor premiss which I therefore deny, and when they 4 'prove' it I say that their 'proof' proves nothing, because Constantine was not in a position to give away the privileges of empire, nor was the church in a position to accept them.[2] And if they stub- 5 bornly insist, my point can be proved in this way: nobody has the right to do things because of an office he holds which are in conflict with that office, otherwise one and the same thing would oppose itself in its own nature, which is impossible; but to divide the empire is in conflict with the office bestowed on the emperor, since his task is to hold mankind in obedience to a single will (its commands and its prohibitions), as can easily be seen from the first book of this treatise; therefore the emperor is not allowed to divide the empire. Thus if certain privileges had been taken away from 6 the empire by Constantine, as they maintain, and had passed into the control of the church, that seamless garment would have been torn which even those who pierced Christ the true God with their

on the path of territorial acquisition. The document which records the 'donation' was exposed as a forgery by Lorenzo Valla on philological grounds only in 1440, but its juridical validity had been debated for centuries; see D. Maffei, *La dona-zione di Costantino nei giuristi medievali*, Milano 1964. Nor was its significance merely theoretical: Boniface VIII, for example, had forced the German Emperor-elect Albert to acknowledge its force; see B. Nardi, 'La "donatio Constantini" e Dante', in *Nel mondo di Dante*, Roma 1944, pp. 119–20. See *Dict.*, pp. 234–5.

[2] Dante's refutation is twofold, turning on the unsuitability of the donor and the unsuitability of the recipient, arguments developed in pars. 5–12 and 13–17 respectively.

7 lance dared not divide.[3] Moreover, just as the church has its foundation, so too the empire has its own. For the foundation of the church is Christ; hence the Apostle in *Corinthians* says: 'For other foundation can no man lay than that is laid, which is Jesus Christ.'[4] He is the rock on which the church is built. But the foundation of

8 the empire is human right. Now I say that, just as the church is not allowed to act against its own foundation, but must always rest upon it, in accordance with those words in the *Song of Solomon*: 'Who is this that cometh up from the wilderness, flowing with delights, leaning upon her beloved?',[5] so too the empire is not allowed to do anything which is in conflict with human right. But if the empire were to destroy itself that would conflict with human

9 right: therefore the empire is not allowed to destroy itself. Therefore since to divide the empire would be to destroy it – for empire consists precisely in the unity of universal monarchy – it is clear that whoever embodies imperial authority is not allowed to divide the empire. For it is clear from what was said earlier that to destroy the empire is in conflict with human right.

10 Moreover, all jurisdiction is prior to the judge who exercises it, for the judge is appointed for the sake of the jurisdiction, and not vice versa; but the empire is a jurisdiction which embraces within its scope every other temporal jurisdiction:[6] therefore it is prior to its judge, who is the emperor, for the emperor is appointed for its sake, and not vice versa. From this it is clear that the emperor, precisely as emperor, cannot change it, because he derives from it

11 the fact that he is what he is. Now I say this: either he was emperor when he is said to have conferred this power on the church, or he was not; if he was not, then it is obvious that he could not give away any part of the empire; if he was, since such a conferring of power would be a lessening of his own jurisdiction, then precisely

12 because he was emperor he could not do it. Besides, if one emperor could cut off some portion of the jurisdiction of the empire, then so could another on the same grounds. And since temporal jurisdic-

---

[3] John 19, 23–4; cf. *Mon.* I, xvi, 3 and n. 5.
[4] 1 Corinthians 3, 11; cf. Ephesians 2, 20; 1 Peter 2, 6.
[5] Song of Solomon 8, 5 (the AV omits the phrase 'flowing with delights').
[6] Cf. Dante's opening definition in *Mon.* I, ii, 2: the two key aspects of that definition (that monarchy is a unity, and that it overrides and encompasses all lower forms of secular authority) underlie the attack on the donation of Constantine.

tion is finite and every finite thing can be destroyed by a finite series of subdivisions, it would follow that the primary jurisdiction could be entirely obliterated; and this is against reason. Again, since a 13 person who gives functions as an agent, and a person who receives as a patient, as Aristotle says in the fourth book of the *Ethics*, for a donation to be legitimate requires a suitable disposition not just in the giver, but in the recipient as well: 'for it seems that the action of active agents is transferred to the "patient" if he is disposed to receive it'.[7] But the church was utterly unsuited to receiving tem- 14 poral things because of the command which expressly forbade it, as we gather from these words in *Matthew*: 'Provide neither gold, nor silver, nor brass in your purses, nor scrip for your journey', etc.[8] For even if in *Luke*[9] we find that this command was relaxed with regard to certain things, yet I have been unable to find that after that prohibition the church was ever granted permission to possess gold and silver. And thus, if the church could not receive 15 it, then even supposing that Constantine had been in a position to perform that action, nonetheless the action itself was not possible because of the unsuitability of the 'patient' or recipient. It is there-fore clear that the church could not accept it as a possession, nor Constantine give it as an irrevocable gift. The emperor could how- 16 ever consign a patrimony and other resources to the guardianship of the church, provided it was without prejudice to the superior imperial authority, whose unity admits no division. And God's vicar 17 could receive it, not as owner but as administrator of its fruits for the church and for Christ's poor, as the apostles are known to have done.[10]

xi

Again they say that Pope Hadrian called on Charlemagne to defend him and the church against the wrongs done by the Longobards at the time of Desiderius their king; and that Charlemagne received the honour of empire from him in spite of the fact that Michael

[7] *Ethics* 4, 1 1120a 14.
[8] Matthew 10, 9–10.
[9] Luke 22, 35–6, as already cited in the previous chapter; cf. Luke 9, 3 and 10, echoing Matthew.
[10] Acts 4, 34–7.

2 was ruling in Constantinople.[1] For this reason they say that all those
who have been emperors of the Romans since his time are defenders
of the church and must be called to office by the church; from this
that dependency which they wish to prove would indeed follow.
3 To demolish this argument I say that they are saying nothing at
all: the usurping of a right does not establish a right. For if it did,
it could be proved in the same way that the authority of the church
is dependent on the emperor, given that the emperor Otto restored
Pope Leo and deposed Benedict and led him into exile in Saxony.[2]

xii

Their argument based on reason runs as follows. Adopting a principle from the tenth book of the *Metaphysics*,[1] they say: all things
belonging to a single species are referred to one thing which is the
measure for all things which belong to that species; but all men
belong to the same species; therefore they are to be referred to one
2 man as their common measure. And since the supreme Pontiff and
the emperor are men, if that conclusion is valid, it must be possible
to refer them to a single man. And since the pope must not be
referred to any other man, it remains that the emperor along with
all other men must be referred to him, as to their measure and rule;
from this too the conclusion they want to reach does indeed follow.
3 To refute this argument I say that, when they say 'Those things
which are of one species must be referred to a single thing of that
species which is the measure for the species', they are correct. And
similarly they are correct when they say that all men belong to a
single species; and again they reach a correct conclusion when from
these premises they infer that all men are to be referred to a single
measure for the species. But when from this conclusion they draw

---

[1] Dante's account is inaccurate on points of detail (Irene not Michael was ruling
in Constantinople when Charlemagne was crowned; the Pope was Leo III not
Hadrian), but this does not affect the logic of his argument. Davis (p. 163, n. 63)
points out that Dante's inaccuracies probably derive from Tolomeo da Lucca.
[2] Pope Leo VIII had been deposed and then expelled by John XII, who was succeeded by Benedict V. The Emperor Otto I subsequently reinstated Leo and
Benedict was exiled to Saxony in 964.
[1] *Metaphysics* 10, 1 1052b 18–19 and 1053a 18–20: Dante here uses the title *Prima
philosophia* (cf. *Met.* 6, 1 and 11, 4); elsewhere (*Mon.* III, xiii, 6) he will call it *De
simpliciter ente*.

their inference concerning the pope and the emperor, they commit the accidental fallacy.[2] To clarify this it must be borne in mind that 4 it is one thing to be a man, another to be pope; and in the same way it is one thing to be a man and another to be emperor, just as it is one thing to be a man and another to be a father and a master. For man is what he is because of his substantial form, by virtue of 5 which he belongs to a species and a genus and is placed in the category 'substance'; whereas a father is what he is because of his accidental form, which consists of a relationship by virtue of which he belongs to a certain species and genus and comes into the category of 'being related to', that is to say 'relationship'.[3] If this were not so, everything would fall within the category 'substance', inasmuch as no accidental form can have autonomous existence without being located in an existing substance; and this is false. Since there- 6 fore pope and emperor are what they are by virtue of certain relationships, i.e. by virtue of papal and imperial office, which are respectively relationships of 'paternity'[4] and of 'lordship', it is clear that pope and emperor must be assigned as pope and emperor to the category of relationship, and as a consequence be referred to something within that category. So I am saying that there is one 7 measure to which they are to be referred as men, and another as pope and emperor. For as men they are to be referred to the perfect man, who is the measure of all the others, and the model, as it were – whoever he might be – of what is most unified in his species, as we can deduce from the end of the *Ethics*.[5] Insofar as they are 8 terms which express a relationship, as is obvious, they are either to be referred one to the other (if one is subordinate to the other, or if they are related to one another within the species by the type of relationship), or else to some third entity to which they are to be referred as to a common unity. But it cannot be maintained that 9 one is subordinated to the other, because if this were the case one

---

[2] i.e. they confuse accident with substance, see *Mon.* III, iv, n. 10.

[3] Being emperor or pope does not alter the fundamental nature of a man as a man, his 'substantial form' [*forma substantialis*] which is common to all human beings; paternity or fatherhood is by contrast an 'accidental form' [*forma accidentalis*] and implies a relationship to others.

[4] The word 'pope' [*Papa*] is related etymologically to 'father' [*pater*], hence is considered to denote a relationship of paternity.

[5] *Ethics* 10, 5 1176a 15–19 [?]: it is difficult to pinpoint the passage Dante had in mind.

would be predicated of the other; and this is false, for we do not say 'the emperor is pope', nor vice versa. Nor can it be said that they are related to one another within the species, for the pope's function is one thing and the emperor's another, precisely because they are pope and emperor; therefore they are to be referred to some other thing in which they find their unity.

10 Consequently it must be grasped that as relationship stands to relationship, so the terms of relationship stand to one another.[6] If therefore papal and imperial office, being relationships of authority, are to be referred to the principle of authority, from which they derive with their differentiating characteristics, then pope and emperor (being the terms of relationship) will be referable to some entity in which it is possible to discern that principle of authority

11 without the other differentiating characteristics. And this will either be God himself, in whom all principles form an absolute unity, or else some entity lower than God, in which the principle of authority, derived from the absolute principle and differentiating itself

12 from it,[7] becomes distinctive and individual. Thus it is evident that pope and emperor, considered as men, are to be referred to one thing; but as pope and emperor they are to be referred to another; and thus the answer to their argument from reason is clear.

xiii

Having stated and ruled out the errors on which those who claim that Roman sovereign authority derives from the Roman Pontiff principally base their case, we must return to demonstrate the truth of the third question we proposed from the beginning to discuss. This truth will emerge with sufficient clarity if, conducting our inquiry in the light of the principle established earlier,[1] I show that the said imperial authority derives directly from the summit of all

2 being, that is from God. And this will be demonstrated whether

---

[6] In concrete terms, as papal office stands to imperial office, so pope stands to emperor.

[7] The best explanation of the phrase 'differentiating itself from it' [*per differentiam superpositionis*], and an unarguable case for its authenticity, is given by Ricci, *EN*, pp. 264–5; see also E. Kantorowicz, *The King's Two Bodies. A Study in Medieval Political Theology*, Princeton 1957, p. 458.

[1] In *Mon.* III, ii, 2.

the church's authority is shown to have no bearing on it – given that there is no quarrel about any other authority – or whether it is proved positively[2] that it derives directly from God. That the 3 authority of the church is not the cause of imperial authority is proved in this way: a thing cannot be the cause of the power of something else if that something else is fully functional when the first thing does not exist or exerts no influence; but the empire had all its authority at a time when the church did not exist or had no influence; therefore the church is not the cause of the empire's power, nor therefore of its authority, since its power and its authority are the same thing. Let the church be A, the empire B, the 4 authority or power of the empire C; if, when A did not yet exist, C was in B, it is impossible for A to be the cause of C's being in B, since it is impossible for an effect to exist before its cause. Besides, if when A is not yet functioning, C is in B, then of necessity A is not the cause of C's being in B, since to produce an effect the cause must operate first (especially the efficient cause,[3] about which we are here speaking). The major premiss of this proof is clear from the 5 terms in which it is formulated;[4] the minor premiss[5] is confirmed by Christ and by the church. Christ confirms it by his birth and his death, as was said earlier; the church when Paul in the *Acts of the Apostles* says to Festus: 'I stand at Caesar's judgment seat, where I ought to be judged';[6] and again when the angel of God said to Paul a little later: 'Fear not, Paul; thou must be brought before Caesar';[7] and again, later, Paul said to the Jews who were in Italy: 'But when the Jews spake against it, I was constrained to appeal unto Caesar, not that I had aught to accuse my nation of, but to deliver my soul from death.'[8] For if Caesar had not at that time had authority to 6 judge temporal matters, Christ would not have assented to this, nor would the angel have pronounced those words, nor would the man

---

[2] i.e. 'probatively', 'affirmatively' [*ostensive*], giving a positive proof and not a proof by default using an argument *per impossibile*; see Aristotle, *Prior Analytics* I, 29; and *Mon.* III, ii, n. 2.
[3] See *Metaphysics* 5, 2; *Mon.* I, ii, n. 3.
[4] i.e. it does not need to be proved, because it is self-evident that 'a thing cannot be the cause. . .' (par. 3).
[5] The minor premiss is that 'the empire had all its authority. . .' (par. 3).
[6] Acts 25, 10.
[7] Acts 27, 24.
[8] Acts 28, 19; Psalms 32, 19 (AV 33, 19); Joshua 2, 13.

who said 'I desire to depart and to be with Christ' have been appeal-
7 ing to a competent judge.[9] Indeed if Constantine had not had authority, he could not legitimately have handed over into the church's
guardianship those things of the empire's which he did hand over;
and thus the church would benefit by that donation unjustly, since
God wishes offerings to be spotless, in accordance with the words
of *Leviticus*: 'No offering, which ye shall bring unto the lord, shall
8 be made with leaven.'[10] For although this commandment appears
to be addressed to those who make an offering, nonetheless by
implication it refers also to the recipients; for it is foolish to think
that God would wish that something should be received which he
has forbidden should be offered, since in the same book he commands the Levites: 'Neither shall ye make yourselves unclean with
9 them, that ye should be defiled thereby.'[11] But to say that the church
misuses the patrimony entrusted to it in this way is most improper;
the proposition from which this followed is therefore false.

xiv

Moreover, if the church had the power to confer authority on the
Roman Prince, it would have it either from God, or from itself, or
from some emperor, or from the consent of all men or at least the
most exceptional among them; there is no other channel by which
this power could have flowed to the church; but it does not derive
2 it from any of these; therefore it does not have the said power. That
it does not derive it from any of these can be shown as follows.
For if it had received it from God, this would have been either by
divine law or by natural law, because what comes from nature comes
3 from God, although the converse is not true. But it did not come
by natural law, because nature imposes laws only on its own effects,
since when God brings something into being without secondary
agents[1] he cannot be less than perfect. Thus, since the church is
not an effect of nature, but of God who said: 'Upon this rock I
will build my church',[2] and elsewhere: 'I have finished the work

---

[9] Philippians 1, 23; cf. *Mon.* II, xi on the authority of the judge.
[10] Leviticus 2, 11.
[11] Leviticus 11, 43.
[1] i.e. directly, not using nature as an intermediary; cf. *Mon.* II, iv, 1 on miracles.
[2] Matthew 16, 18.

which thou gavest me to do',[3] it is apparent that it is not nature which gave its law to the church. But it did not come by divine law either, for the whole of divine law is encompassed within the two Testaments, and I am quite unable to find in them that involvement in or concern for temporal things was recommended to the first or the later priesthood. On the contrary I find that the first priests were expressly enjoined to keep aloof from such involvement, as is clear from God's words to Moses;[4] as were the priests of the new order in Christ's words to his disciples;[5] freedom from such involvement would not be possible if the authority of temporal power flowed from the priesthood, since at the very least it would have had the responsibility for taking action to confer authority, and then for continual watchfulness lest the person on whom authority had been conferred deviate from the path of righteousness. That the church did not receive this power from itself can easily be proved. There is nothing which can give what it does not possess; and so every agent must be in actuality like the thing which it intends to produce, as we see from the *Metaphysics*.[6] But it is clear that if the church gave itself that power, it did not have it before it gave it; and thus it would have given itself what it did not possess, which is impossible. That it did not receive it from some emperor is sufficiently clear from what was proved earlier.[7] And who can doubt that it did not receive it from the consent of all men or of the most exceptional among them, given that not only all Asians and Africans, but also the greater part of those who live in Europe find the idea abhorrent? It is tedious to offer proofs in matters which are self-evident.[8]

XV

Equally, whatever is in conflict with the nature of a thing is not to be numbered among its powers, since the powers of each thing

---

[3] John 17, 4.
[4] Numbers 18, 20 (but God is here speaking to Aaron, not to Moses); Deuteronomy 18, 1–2.
[5] Matthew 10, 9–10; 6, 19f.
[6] *Metaphysics* 9, 8 (cf. 7, 7); cf. *Mon.* I, xiii, 3.
[7] In ch. x.
[8] Cf. *Mon.* I, i, 4.

come from its nature and serve to achieve its purpose; but the power to confer authority on the realm of our mortality is in conflict with the nature of the church; therefore it is not to be numbered among

2 its powers. To clarify the minor premiss it must be borne in mind that the church's nature is the form of the church; for although 'nature' is used with reference to matter and to form, nonetheless

3 it refers first and foremost to form, as is shown in the *Physics*.[1] Now the 'form' of the church is simply the life of Christ, including both his words and his deeds; for his life was the model and exemplar for the church militant, especially for the pastors, and above all for the supreme pastor, whose task is to feed the lambs and the sheep.[2]

4 Hence he himself says, in *John*, leaving the 'form' of his life: 'I have given you an example, that ye should do as I have done to you';[3] and he said to Peter in particular, after bestowing on him the office of pastor, as we read in the same Gospel: 'Peter, follow

5 me.'[4] But Christ renounced this kind of kingdom in the presence of Pilate, saying: 'My kingdom is not of this world; if my kingdom were of this world, then would my servants fight, that I should not be delivered to the Jews; but now is my kingdom not from hence.'[5]

6 Which is not to be understood to mean that Christ, who is God, is not Lord of this kingdom, for the Psalmist says 'The sea is his, and he made it: and his hands formed the dry land';[6] but that, as

7 the model for the church, he had no concern for this kingdom. Just as if a gold seal were to say, speaking of itself: 'I am not the measure for any class of things'; the statement would not refer to the fact of its being gold, for gold is the measure for the class of metals, but would rather refer to the fact that it is a particular image which

8 can be reproduced by exerting pressure. Thus the 'form' of the church requires that it should speak in this same way and feel in this same way;[7] for it to say or to feel the opposite would be in conflict with its form, as is apparent, that is to say with its nature,

9 which is the same thing. From this we deduce that the power to confer authority on this earthly kingdom is in conflict with the

[1] *Physics* 2, 1 (Dante uses the title *De naturali auditu*).
[2] John 21, 16f.
[3] John 13, 15.
[4] John 21, 19.
[5] John 18, 36.
[6] Psalms 94, 5 (AV 95, 5).
[7] i.e. in the same way as Christ, as reflected in his words cited in par. 5.

nature of the church; for conflict which emerges in a thought or in a statement derives from a conflict which exists in the thing which is thought about or spoken of,[8] just as the truth or falsehood of a statement derives from the fact that the thing referred to is or is not the case, as we are taught in the *Categories*.[9] Thus we have 10 sufficiently proved with the above arguments, by a reduction to the absurd,[10] that the authority of the empire in no way derives from the church.

xvi

Although in the previous chapter it was shown by a *reductio ad absurdum*[1] that the authority of the empire does not derive from the authority of the supreme Pontiff, nonetheless we have not given a complete proof[2] that it derives directly from God, except insofar as that follows as a consequence – the consequence being precisely that if it does not derive from God's vicar, it derives from God. Therefore, to complete the task we set ourselves, we must give a 2 'positive'[3] proof that the emperor, or world ruler, is directly dependent on the prince of the universe, who is God. In order to under- 3 stand this it must be borne in mind that man alone among created beings is the link between corruptible and incorruptible things; and thus he is rightly compared by philosophers to the horizon, which is the link between the two hemispheres.[4] For if he is considered 4 in terms of each of his essential constituent parts, that is soul and body, man is corruptible; if he is considered only in terms of one, his soul, he is incorruptible. Hence the appositeness of Aristotle's remark when he said of the soul, as being incorruptible, in the second book of the *De anima*: 'And it alone, being immortal, can

---

[8] i.e. words and feelings reflect an underlying reality, thus if the church were to speak or feel in a way which is in conflict with Christ's words, it would *be* in conflict with Christ and hence with its own nature.

[9] *Categories* 12, 14b 18–22; cf. *Summule* III, 30 [*Ab eo enim quod res est vel non est, oratio vera vel falsa dicitur*].

[10] The absurdity is that if his adversaries' argument were correct the church would be required to act against its own nature.

[1] See *Mon.* III, xv, n. 10.

[2] A complete proof must include the 'ostensive' or positive proof Dante will now develop in this final chapter.

[3] See *Mon.* III, xiii, n. 2.

[4] Cf. *Liber de causis* 2a.

5 be separated from the corruptible.'[5] Thus if man is a kind of link between corruptible and incorruptible things, since every such link shares something of the nature of the extremes it unites, man must 6 necessarily have something of both natures. And since every nature is ordered towards its own ultimate goal, it follows that man's goal is twofold: so that, just as he alone among all created beings shares in incorruptibility and corruptibility, so he alone among all created beings is ordered to two ultimate goals, one of them being his goal as a corruptible being, the other his goal as an incorruptible being.

7 Ineffable providence has thus set before us two goals to aim at: i.e. happiness in this life, which consists in the exercise of our own powers and is figured in the earthly paradise; and happiness in the eternal life, which consists in the enjoyment of the vision of God (to which our own powers cannot raise us except with the help of 8 God's light) and which is signified by the heavenly paradise. Now these two kinds of happiness must be reached by different means, as representing different ends. For we attain the first through the teachings of philosophy, provided that we follow them putting into practice the moral and intellectual virtues;[6] whereas we attain the second through spiritual teachings which transcend human reason, provided that we follow them putting into practice the theological 9 virtues, i.e. faith, hope and charity. These ends and the means to attain them have been shown to us on the one hand by human reason, which has been entirely revealed to us by the philosophers, and on the other by the Holy Spirit, who through the prophets and sacred writers, through Jesus Christ the son of God, coeternal with him, and through his disciples, has revealed to us the transcendent truth we cannot do without; yet human greed would cast these ends and means aside if men, like horses, prompted to wander by their animal natures, were not held in check 'with bit and bridle'[7] on 10 their journey.[8] It is for this reason that man had need of two guides corresponding to his twofold goal: that is to say the supreme Pontiff, to lead mankind to eternal life in conformity with revealed truth, and the emperor, to guide mankind to temporal happiness in con- 11 formity with the teachings of philosophy. And since none can reach

[5] *De anima* 2, 2 413b 26.
[6] See *Mon.* II, vii, 4 (and n. 3).
[7] Psalms 31, 9 (AV 32, 9).
[8] i.e. in this life, the journey of this mortal life on earth.

this harbour (or few, and these few with great difficulty) unless the waves of seductive greed are calmed and the human race rests free in the tranquillity of peace, this is the goal which the protector of the world, who is called the Roman Prince, must strive with all his might to bring about: i.e. that life on this threshing-floor[9] of mortals may be lived freely and in peace. And since the disposition of this 12 world is a result of the disposition inherent in the circling of the heavens, in order that useful teachings concerning freedom and peace can be applied appropriately to times and places, it is necessary for provision for this protector to be made by Him who takes in at a glance the whole disposition of the heavens. For he alone is the one who preordained this disposition, making provision through it to bind all things in due order. If this is so, then God alone 13 chooses, he alone confirms, since he has none above him. From this it can be further deduced that neither those who are now called 'electors',[10] nor others who in whatever way have been so called, should be given this name; rather they should be thought of as 'proclaimers of divine providence'. Thus it happens that those 14 granted the honour of making this proclamation may sometimes disagree among themselves, either because all of them or because some of them, their understanding clouded by the fog of greed, fail to perceive what God's dispensation is. Thus it is evident then that 15 the authority of the temporal monarch flows down into him without any intermediary from the Fountainhead of universal authority; this Fountainhead, though one in the citadel of its own simplicity of nature,[11] flows into many streams from the abundance of his goodness.

And now it seems to me that I have reached the goal I set myself. 16 For the truth has been revealed[12] concerning the first question we were inquiring into: whether the office of monarch was necessary to the well-being of the world; and to the second point of inquiry:

---

[9] The threshing-floor or small patch of earth [*areola*] is the inhabitable land mass of the Northern hemisphere; the choice of word emphasizes the insignificance of human life seen in the perspective of the cosmic order.

[10] i.e. the German princes who elected the Emperor.

[11] The phrase 'the citadel of its own simplicity of nature' [*in arce sue simplicitatis*], and the contrast between unity and multiplicity, echo Boethius, *De consolatione philosophiae* 4, prose 6 [*in suae simplicitatis arce*].

[12] Cf. *Mon.* I, i, 5. We have come full circle, the truth announced in the opening chapter of the treatise has been revealed [*enucleata*].

whether the Roman people took on empire by right; and to the last point of inquiry: whether the authority of the monarch comes from 17 God directly or from someone else. But the truth concerning this last question should not be taken so literally as to mean that the Roman Prince is not in some sense subject to the Roman Pontiff, since this earthly happiness is in some sense ordered towards 18 immortal happiness. Let Caesar therefore show that reverence towards Peter which a firstborn son should show his father, so that, illumined by the light of paternal grace, he may the more effectively light up the world, over which he has been placed by Him alone who is ruler over all things spiritual and temporal.

Biographical notes

These notes are intended to provide the reader with a modicum of information about the authors and texts cited by Dante in the *Monarchy*. Titles marked with an asterisk (*) are referred to explicitly in the treatise. The list does not include the books of the Bible; these appear in a separate Table on pp. 99–101.

AQUINAS, Saint Thomas. Scholastic theologian and philosopher (1225/6–1274). Educated at Monte Cassino near his birthplace in Southern Italy, and then at Naples, he became a Dominican, and studied with Albert the Great in Cologne and Paris; he subsequently taught in both cities as well as in Rome, Bologna and Naples. Author of the *Summa theologiae*, the *Summa contra Gentiles* and *Commentaries* on many of Aristotle's texts, in which he sought to reconcile the teachings of the Greek philosopher with the revealed truths of the Christian religion. Canonized in 1323, two years after Dante's death.

ARISTOTLE, Greek philosopher (384 BC–322 BC). A pupil of Plato in Athens, on his return to Macedonia he became tutor to Alexander the Great; later he returned to Athens and founded the Peripatetic school of philosophy. Author of treatises on logic [*Categories, *Prior Analytics, *Sophistical Refutations*], natural science [*Physics, *De anima*], rhetoric, *Metaphysics, *Ethics, and *Politics*: these works, translated and interpreted in later centuries – firstly into and in Arabic by Moslem scholars and subsequently (in the twelfth and thirteenth centuries) into and in Latin – formed the basis of philosophic and scientific learning in the late medieval Christian world.

95

The pseudo-Aristotelian *De causis* [or *Liber de causis*], which derives from the *Institutio* of Proclus and which was a key text for the transmission of neo-Platonic ideas to the Middle Ages, is cited by Dante with no indication of authorship.

AUGUSTINE, Saint. One of the great church fathers (354–430). Born in North Africa of a pagan father and a devout Christian mother; after a dissolute early life he was converted and baptized under the influence of St Ambrose in Milan (387); in the closing decades of his life he was bishop of Hippo in North Africa. Author, among other works, of the immensely influential *Confessions*, the *De civitate Dei*, and the *De doctrina christiana*.

AVERROES, Moslem philosopher, scholar, lawyer and doctor (1126–1198). Born in Cordoba, he died in Morocco. His most famous work was a commentary on Aristotle (whose writings he knew in Arabic translation); this was translated into Latin before 1250. His *Commentary on the De anima* in particular, with its unorthodox view of human intellect, was a controversial text for scholastic theologians.

BOETHIUS, Roman philosopher and statesman (*c.* AD 480–AD 524). His *De consolatione philosophiae*, written in prison in Pavia while he was awaiting execution for allegedly having plotted against King Theodoric, was a key text for Dante in both its philosophical content and its literary form, which combined meditative expository prose and sustained verse composition.

CICERO, Marcus Tullius. Roman writer, philosopher and statesman (106 BC–43 BC). Author, among other works, of the *De fine bonorum* [i.e. *De finibus*], *De inventione*, *De officiis*.

DANTE (*see* Principal events, pp. xxxix–xlii). The cross-reference to the *Divine Comedy* is a self-citation not untypical of this most self-conscious and self-referential of writers.

EUCLID, Greek mathematician (lived *c.* 300 BC). Author of the *Elements of Geometry*.

GALEN, physician (*c.* AD 130–*c.* AD 200). Born at Pergamum in Asia Minor, where he studied medicine, he later moved to Rome, where he became very famous, and included emperors among his patients;

after Hippocrates he was the most celebrated physician of antiquity. A prolific writer on medical subjects, his texts were authoritative throughout the Middle Ages and until the sixteenth century.

JUVENAL, Roman satirist (*c.* AD 60–*c.* AD 140). Author of sixteen Satires [*VIII], which Dante seems to have known and to quote only at second hand.

LIVY, Roman historian (59 BC–AD 17). Born at Padua, where he also died, he lived most of his life at Rome. Author of a lengthy history of Rome from the foundation of the city to 9 BC, *Ab urbe condita*; only 35 of the original 142 books are now extant, but the work was frequently abridged in the Middle Ages, and these abridged versions (which may be Dante's source) cover most of the missing material.

LUCAN, Roman poet (AD 39–AD 65). A nephew of Seneca, the Stoic philosopher and tragedian; born in Spain, he was brought up in Rome, where he took his own life in his twenty-sixth year on the order of Nero, against whom he had conspired. Author of the *De bello civili*, also known as the *Pharsalia*, an epic poem on the civil war recounting the struggles between Caesar and Pompey.

MASTER OF THE SENTENCES (*see* Peter Lombard).

MASTER OF THE SIX PRINCIPLES. The author of a *Commentary on Aristotle's *Categories*.

OROSIUS, Spanish historian and priest. A contemporary and friend of Saint Augustine, on whose suggestion he wrote his *Seven Books of History against the Pagans*, which trace the history of the world from a Christian viewpoint, in order to show that there has been no decline in civilization since the coming of Christianity. This work served later generations as a source book not only for ancient history but also for geography.

OVID, Roman poet (43 BC–AD 17). Author, among other works, of the *Metamorphoses*, Dante's chief source for classical mythology.

PETER LOMBARD (*c.* 1095–1160). Also known as the Master of the Sentences from the title of his work *Libri quattuor sententiarum*, a collection of 'sentences' or opinions of the Church Fathers, which became enormously popular and was used as a theological text-book.

PYTHAGORAS, Greek philosopher (*c.* 582 BC–*c.* 506 BC). His thought centred on the idea of number and the importance of the numerical and mathematical relations between things. No writings of his are extant; Dante's knowledge of his doctrines came principally from Aristotle.

SENECA, Roman philosopher and dramatist (4 BC–AD 65). Dante, like his contemporaries, mistakenly believed him to be the author of the *De quattuor virtutibus*, a work now attributed to St Martin of Dumio, who died in 580.

THOMAS (*see* Aquinas).

VEGETIUS, Roman writer. Author of the *De re militari*, a study of the art of warfare and military strategy.

VIRGIL, Roman poet (70 BC–19 BC). Author of the *Eclogues*, the *Georgics*, and the *Aeneid*, an epic poem which traces the legendary pre-history of the Roman people from the fall of Troy to the victory of Aeneas over Turnus on the spot which is destined to become the city of Rome and the seat of the Roman empire.

Table of biblical citations*

Old Testament

Genesis
[1, 16 – III, i, 5]
1, 16 – III, iv, 2
1, 19 and 31 – III, iv, 13
1, 26 – I, viii, 2
27, 1f. – I, xiii, 4
29, 34–5 – III, v, 1

Exodus
2, 14 – II, xi, 4
7 – II, vii, 8
8, 16–19 – II, iv, 2
18, 13–26 (and Deuteronomy 1, 9–18) – I, xiv, 9

Leviticus
2, 11 – III, xiii, 7
11, 43 – III, xiii, 8
17, 3 – II, vii, 5

Numbers
18, 20 (and Deuteronomy 18, 1–2) – III, xiv, 5

Deuteronomy
6, 4 (and Mark 12, 29) – I, viii, 3

Joshua
[2, 13 – III, xiii, 5]

1 Regum (AV 1 Samuel)
10, 1 and 15 and 16, 13 – III, vi, 1
17, 4–51 – II, ix, 11
15 – II, vii, 8

2 Chronicles
20, 12 – II, vii, 8

Psalms
1, 3 – I, i, 2
2, 1–3 – II, i, 1
4, 8 (AV 4, 7) – I, xv, 3
8, 6 (AV 8, 5) – I, iv, 2
10, 8 (AV 11, 7) – II, ix, 1
[31, 9 (AV 32, 9) – III, xvi, 9]
[32, 19 (AV 33, 19) – III, xiii, 5]
49, 16 (AV 50, 16) – I, xiii, 5

* References in square brackets indicate a clear biblical allusion (e.g. to the buried talent, or the seamless garment, or the many-headed beast), to whose biblical source Dante does not explicitly draw attention.

99

71, 1 (AV 72, 1) – I, xiii, 7
94, 5 (AV 95, 5) – III, xv, 6
110, 9 (AV 111, 9) – III, iii, 12
111, 7 (AV 112, 6–7) – III, i, 4
132, 1 (AV 133, 1) – I, xvi, 5

Proverbs
8, 7 – III, i, 3

Song of Solomon
1, 3 – III, iii, 12
8, 5 – III, x, 8

Isaiah
6, 6–7 – III, i, 3
53, 4 – II, xi, 5

Daniel
6, 22 – III, i, 1

New Testament

Matthew
2, 1–13 – III, vii, 1
7, 2 (and Luke 6, 38) – II, iii, 5
10, 9–10 – III, x, 14 and III, xiv, 5
10, 34–5 – III, ix, 18
12, 25 (and Luke 11, 17) – I, v, 8
14, 28 – III, ix, 12
15, 1–3 – III, iii, 15
16, 15–16 – III, ix, 10
16, 18 – III, xiv, 3
16, 19 – III, viii, 1
16, 21–3 – III, ix, 10
17, 3–4 – III, ix, 11
18, 20 – II, ix, 5
[25, 14–30 – I, i, 3]
26, 31–5 – III, ix, 13
28, 20 – III, iii, 13

Mark
12, 29 (and Deuteronomy 6, 4) – I, viii, 3
14, 29–31 – III, ix, 14

Luke
2, 1 – I, xvi, 2
2, 1 – II, viii, 14
2, 1 – II, x, 6
2, 14 – I, iv, 3

22, 7 – III, ix, 3
22, 14 – III, ix, 4
22, 33–4 – III, ix, 14
22, 35–6 – III, ix, 5 and III, x, 14
22, 38 – III, ix, 1
23, 11 – II, xi, 6
24, 36 (and John 20, 21) – I, iv, 4

John
1, 3 – II, ii, 4
[8, 44 – III, iii, 8]
10, 9 – II, vii, 6
11, 49–52 and 18, 14 – II, xi, 6
13, 6–8 – III, ix, 15
13, 15 – III, xv, 4
17, 4 – III, xiv, 3
18, 10 (and Matthew 26, 51–2; Mark 14, 47; Luke 22, 50–2) – III, ix, 16
18, 36 – III, xv, 5
[19, 23–4 – I, xvi, 3 and III, x, 6]
19, 30 – II, xi, 3
20, 4–6 – III, ix, 16
21, 7 – III, ix, 16
[21, 16f. – III, xv, 3]

21, 19 – III, xv, 4
22, 21 – III, ix, 16

Acts of the Apostles
1, 1 – III, ix, 19
1, 26 – II, vii, 9
[4, 34–7 – III, x, 17]
25, 10 – III, xiii, 5
27, 24 – III, xiii, 5
28, 19 – III, xiii, 5

Romans
1, 20 – II, ii, 8
5, 12 – II, xi, 2
[8, 17 – III, iii, 10]
11, 33 – II, viii, 10

1 Corinthians
3, 11 (cf. Ephesians 2, 20 and 1
Peter 2, 6) – III, x, 7
[9, 24 – I, i, 5]

Galatians
4, 4 – I, xvi, 2

Ephesians
2, 3 – II, xi, 2
1, 5–8 – II, xi, 3

Philippians
1, 23 – III, xiii, 6

Colossians
[1, 13 – III, i, 3]

1 Thessalonians
5, 8 – III, i, 3

2 Timothy
4, 8 – II, ix, 19

Hebrews
11, 6 – II, vii, 5

James
1, 5 – I, i, 6

2 Peter
[1, 21 – III, iv, 11]

Revelation
[12, 3 and 17, 9 – I, xvi, 4]

Table of explicit citations of Aristotle[*]

Ethics

1, 2 1094b 9–11 – II, vii, 3
1, 3 1094b 23–5 and 7 1098a
  25–8 – II, ii, 7
1, 6 1096a 13–5 – III, i, 3
1, 7 1098b 6–7 – I, iii, 1
4, 1 1120a 14 – III, x, 13
5, 1 1129a 32–b10 and 2 1130a
  16–32 – I, xi, 11
5, 1 1129b 28–9 – I, xi, 5
5, 10 1137a 31–1138a 2 – I, xiv, 4
6, 9 1142b 22–4 – II, v, 23
7, 1 1145a 20–3 – II, iii, 9
10, 1 – I, xiii, 4
10, 1 1172a 34–5 – II, x, 6
10, 5 1176a 15–9 [?] – III, xii, 7
10, 9 1179b 32f. – I, xv, 9

Politics

1, 2 1252a 31 – I, iii, 10
1, 2 1252b 20 – I, v, 5
1, 2 1253a 25–39 – II, vii, 2
1, 5 – I, iv, 2

1, 5 1254a 21–4 and 5 1255a 1–2;
  6 1255b 5–9 – II, vi, 7
3, 4 – I, xii, 10
4, 1 1289a 13–15 – I, xii, 11
4, 8 1294a 21–2 – II, iii, 4

Physics

1, 3 186a 6f. – III, iv, 4
2, 1 – III, xv, 2
2, 2 – I, ix, 1
2, 2 194a 28–31 – II, vi, 5

Metaphysics

1, 2 982b 25–6 – I, xii, 8
1, 5 986a 15 – b 2 – I, xv, 2
9, 8 – III, xiv, 6
9, 8 1049b 24–6 – I, xiii, 3
10, 1 1052b 18–9 and 1053a
  18–20 – III, xii, 1
10, 2 1053b 20–8 and 1054a 9–13 –
  I, xv, 2
12, 10 – I, x, 6

[*] There are of course many direct echoes of Aristotle's thinking central to Dante's argument whose Aristotelian derivation is not explicitly acknowledged as such in the text (e.g. the notion of the good life, the three forms of just and perverted government, the conception of justice as a virtue which operates in relation to other people, and so on).

103

De anima
2, 2 413b 26 – III, xvi,
  4
3 – I, iii, 9

Categories
12, 14b 18–22 – III, xv, 9

Prior Analytics
1, 25 41b 36f. – III, vii, 3

Sophistical Refutations
18, 176b 29 – III, iv, 4

Rhetoric
1, 1 – I, xi, 11

Index

Abidos 52
abscess 71
absurd, reduction to the 91
accidental (as opposed to substantial) 85
accidents, accidental properties
    [*accidentia*] 71
Acts of the Apostles 49, 87
action, actions 8, 17, 22, 45, 80, 83
  a miracle is a direct action by the
    First Cause 37–8
  human 49, 81
  in every action the primary aim of the
    agent is to reproduce its own
    likeness 22
  more telling than words 22, 59
  of an agent 16
  of the supreme Pontiff and the
    Emperor 69
activity [*operatio*], *see also* function
  proper to a given nature 6
  specific to humanity as a whole 6, 8
actualization 7, *see also* perfection,
  realization
Adam
  one of our first parents 28
  sin of 60
administrator 83
advantage, personal 40, 42, 71
adversary 71
Adversary, that ancient 55
Aeacidae, the 55
Aeneas
  father of the Romans 47, 56
  most glorious king 34

Aeneid 34, 56, *see also* Virgil, poet
affections 29
Africa 35, 36, 43
Africans 57, 89
Agathon 74
agent, agents 18, 22, 23, 83, 89, *see also*
  patient
  action of active agent is transferred to
    the 'patient' 83
  free agents 41
  secondary agents 38, 88
agreement necessary for trial by combat
  54
Albans 56
Alexander 52
allies 41
alms-giving 45
amazement 30, 33, 43, *see also*
  astonishment
ambassadors 52, 55
ambition 51
ancestors 34, 42, *see also* forebears
  of Aeneas 35
Anchises 47
ancients, their testimony to the nobility
  of the Romans 34
Andromache 36
angel, angels 8, 66, *see also* intelligences
  and beings, non-material
  of God 87
anger 66
angles 19
animal, animals
  'animal' as consequent 44, 73

revenues of the church 58
reverence, Dante's 68
rewards commensurate with deserts 34
riches 52, 61
right 56, 84
  basis of 46
  definition of 40
  does not extend beyond the capacity
    to exercise it 46
  essence and purpose of 40
  exists firstly in the mind of God 32
  hereditary 35
  human right the foundation of empire
    82
  is divine will 32
  is what is in harmony with divine will
    33
  limits of 46
  true and pure 33
rights, public 70
righteousness [*iustitia*] 22, 63, *see also*
  justice
righteousness [*rectitudo*], path of 89
rite, pagan 38
rival, rivals 52, 53
rock on which the church is built 82, 88
Roman people, the *passim*
  came to empire by right 33, 47
  father of 37
  noblest 34
  ordained by nature to rule 47
  that glorious people (i.e. the Romans)
    33
  that holy, dutiful and glorious people
    (i.e. the Romans) 40
Romans, the 52, 56, 57, 84
Rome 42, 47, 52, 57
  name of 38
  nobility of 39
route 20, 24, 70
rule [*regula*], justice a kind of 15
ruler, rulers 12, 13, 14, 15, 22, 23, 24,
  25, 27, 30, 74, 75, 91
  over all things spiritual and temporal
    94
rules of warfare 57

Sabines 57
sacrifice of Cato 43
salutation of Christ 9
salvation of mankind 28
Samnites 57

Samuel 49, 73
sand 53
Satan 79
Saturn 15
Saul 49, 73
Saviour 9, 58
Saxony 84
sceptre 41, 52, 73
sciences 5
Scipio 57
scorn 31, *see also* derision
scrip 78, 83
Scriptures 49, 68, 69, 70, *see also* Gospel
Scythians 24, 51, 66
seal 33, 90
sea, seas 53, 80, 90
self-sufficiency 10
self-sacrifice 48
Semiramis 51
senate 41
Seneca 40
seniority 73
sense
  allegorical 69
  mystical 70
  not to be taken in an absolute sense
    76
seraphim 63
servant, servants 21, 79, 90
service
  acts of 41
  public 41
Sestos 52
shadows
  of death 43
  of night 38
shame 63
sheep 68, 90
shepherd, shepherds 8, 58, 66, 68
shield, shields 38
shipwrecks 28
shoes 78
sick in both intellects 28
sign, signs
  clear 33
  external 41
  God's will revealed by a sign 49
  indubitable 41
  of the working of divine providence
    30
  universal sign [*in logic*] 76, 77
silence 58

Cambridge Texts in the History of Political Thought

Titles published in the series thus far

Aristotle *The Politics* and *The Constitution of Athens* (edited by Stephen Everson)
  0 521 48400 6 paperback
Arnold *Culture and Anarchy and other writings* (edited by Stefan Collini)
  0 521 37796 x paperback
Astell *Political Writings* (edited by Patricia Springborg)
  0 521 42845 9 paperback
Augustine *The City of God against the Pagans* (edited by R. W. Dyson)
  0 521 46843 4 paperback
Austin *The Province of Jurisprudence Determined* (edited by Wilfrid E. Rumble)
  0 521 44756 9 paperback
Bacon *The History of the Reign of King Henvy VII* (edited by Brian Vickers)
  0 521 58663 1 paperback
Bakunin *Statism and Anarchy* (edited by Marshall Shatz)
  0 521 36973 8 paperback
Baxter *A Holy Commonwealth* (edited by William Lamont)
  0 521 40580 7 paperback
Bayle *Political Writings* (edited by Sally L. Jenkinson)
  0 521 47677 1 paperback
Beccaria *On Crimes and Punishments and other writings* (edited by Richard Bellamy)
  0 521 47982 7 paperback
Bentham *A Fragment on Government* (introduction by Ross Harrison)
  0 521 35929 5 paperback
Bernstein *The Preconditions of Socialism* (edited by Henry Tudor)
  0 521 39808 8 paperback
Bodin *On Sovereignty* (edited by Julian H. Franklin)
  0 521 34992 3 paperback
Bolingbroke *Political Writings* (edited by David Armitage)
  0 521 58697 6 paperback
Bossuet *Politics Drawn from the Very Words of Holy Scripture* (edited by Patrick Riley)
  0 521 36807 3 paperback
The British Idealists (edited by David Boucher)
  0 521 45951 6 paperback
Burke *Pre-Revolutionary Writings* (edited by Ian Harris)
  0 521 36800 6 paperback
Christine De Pizan *The Book of the Body Politic* (edited by Kate Langdon Forhan)
  0 521 42259 0 paperback
Cicero *On Duties* (edited by M. T. Griffin and E. M. Atkins)
  0 521 34835 8 paperback
Cicero *On the Commonwealth and On Laws* (edited by James E. G. Zetzel)
  0 521 45959 1 paperback

Comte *Early Political Writings* (edited by H. S. Jones)
    0 521 46923 6 paperback
Conciliarism and Papalism (edited by J. H. Burns and Thomas M. Izbicki)
    0 521 47674 7 paperback
Constant *Political Writings* (edited by Biancamaria Fontana)
    0 521 31632 4 paperback
Dante *Monarchy* (edited by Prue Shaw)
    0 521 56781 5 paperback
Diderot *Political Writings* (edited by John Hope Mason and Robert Wokler)
    0 521 36911 8 paperback
The Dutch Revolt (edited by Martin van Gelderen)
    0 521 39809 6 paperback
The Early Political Writings of the German Romantics (edited by
    Frederick C. Beiser)
    0 521 44951 0 paperback
Early Greek Political Thought from Homer to the Sophists (edited by **Michael Gagarin**
    and Paul Woodruff)
    0 521 43768 7 paperback
The English Levellers (edited by Andrew Sharp)
    0 521 62511 4 paperback
Erasmus *The Education of a Christian Prince* (edited by Lisa Jardine)
    0 521 58811 1 paperback
Fenelon *Telemachus* (edited by Patrick Riley)
    0 521 45662 2 paperback
Ferguson *An Essay on the History of Civil Society* (edited by Fania Oz-Salzberger)
    0 521 44736 4 paperback
Filmer *Patriarcha and Other Writings* (edited by Johann P. Sommerville)
    0 521 39903 3 paperback
Fletcher *Political Works* (edited by John Robertson)
    0 521 43994 9 paperback
Sir John Fortescue *On the Laws and Governance of England* (edited by
    Shelley Lockwood)
    0 521 58996 7 paperback
Fourier *The Theory of the Four Movements* (edited by Gareth Stedman Jones and
    Ian Patterson)
    0 521 35693 8 paperback
Gramsci *Pre-Prison Writings* (edited by Richard Bellamy)
    0 521 42307 4 paperback
Guicciardini *Dialogue on the Government of Florence* (edited by Alison Brown)
    0 521 45623 1 paperback
Harrington *A Commonwealth of Oceana* and *A System of Politics* (edited by
    J. G. A. Pocock)
    0 521 42329 5 paperback

Hegel *Elements of the Philosophy of Right* (edited by Allen W. Wood and H. B. Nisbet)
    0 521 34888 9 paperback
Hegel *Political Writings* (edited by Laurence Dickey and H. B. Nisbet)
    0 521 45979 3 paperback
Hobbes *On the Citizen* (edited by Michael Silverthorne and Richard Tuck)
    0 521 43780 6 paperback
Hobbes *Leviathan* (edited by Richard Tuck)
    0 521 56797 1 paperback
Hobhouse *Liberalism and Other Writings* (edited by James Meadowcroft)
    0 521 43726 1 paperback
Hooker *Of the Laws of Ecclesiastical Polity* (edited by A. S. McGrade)
    0 521 37908 3 paperback
Hume *Political Essays* (edited by Knud Haakonssen)
    0 521 46639 3 paperback
King James VI and I *Political Writings* (edited by Johann P. Sommerville)
    0 521 44729 1 paperback
Jefferson *Political Writings* (edited by Joyce Appleby and Terence Ball)
    0 521 64841 6 paperback
John of Salisbury *Policraticus* (edited by Cary Nederman)
    0 521 36701 8 paperback
Kant *Political Writings* (edited by H. S. Reiss and H. B. Nisbet)
    0 521 39837 1 paperback
Knox *On Rebellion* (edited by Roger A. Mason)
    0 521 39988 2 paperback
Kropotkin *The Conquest of Bread and other writings* (edited by Marshall Shatz)
    0 521 45990 7 paperback
Lawson *Politica sacra et civilis* (edited by Conal Condren)
    0 521 39248 9 paperback
Leibniz *Political Writings* (edited by Patrick Riley)
    0 521 35899 X paperback
The Levellers (edited by Andrew Sharp)
    0 521 62511 4 paperback
Locke *Political Essays* (edited by Mark Goldie)
    0 521 47861 8 paperback
Locke *Two Treatises of Government* (edited by Peter Laslett)
    0 521 35730 6 paperback
Loyseau *A Treatise of Orders and Plain Dignities* (edited by Howell A. Lloyd)
    0 521 45624 X paperback
Luther and Calvin on Secular Authority (edited by Harro Höpfl)
    0 521 34986 9 paperback
Machiavelli *The Prince* (edited by Quentin Skinner and Russell Price)
    0 521 34993 1 paperback

de Maistre *Considerations on France* (edited by Isaiah Berlin and Richard Lebrun)
  o 521 46628 8 paperback
Malthus *An Essay on the Principle of Population* (edited by Donald Winch)
  o 521 42972 2 paperback
Marsiglio of Padua *Defensor minor* and *De translatione Imperii* (edited by
  Cary Nederman)
  o 521 40846 6 paperback
Marx *Early Political Writings* (edited by Joseph O'Malley)
  o 521 34994 X paperback
Marx *Later Political Writings* (edited by Terrell Carver)
  o 521 36739 5 paperback
James Mill *Political Writings* (edited by Terence Ball)
  o 521 38748 5 paperback
J. S. Mill *On Liberty*, with *The Subjection of Women* and *Chapters on Socialism*
  (edited by Stefan Collini)
  o 521 37917 2 paperback
Milton *Political Writings* (edited by Martin Dzelzainis)
  o 521 34866 8 paperback
Montesquieu *The Spirit of the Laws* (edited by Anne M. Cohler, Basia Carolyn Miller
  and Harold Samuel Stone)
  o 521 36974 6 paperback
More *Utopia* (edited by George M. Logan and Robert M. Adams)
  o 521 40318 9 paperback
Morris *News from Nowhere* (edited by Krishan Kumar)
  o 521 42233 7 paperback
Nicholas of Cusa *The Catholic Concordance* (edited by Paul E. Sigmund)
  o 521 56773 4 paperback
Nietzsche *On the Genealogy of Morality* (edited by Keith Ansell-Pearson)
  o 521 40610 2 paperback
Paine *Political Writings* (edited by Bruce Kuklick)
  o 521 36678 x paperback
Plato *Statesman* (edited by Julia Annas and Robin Waterfield)
  o 521 44778 X paperback
Price *Political Writings* (edited by D. O. Thomas)
  o 521 40969 1 paperback
Priestley *Political Writings* (edited by Peter Miller)
  o 521 42561 1 paperback
Proudhon *What is Property?* (edited by Donald R. Kelley and
  Bonnie G. Smith)
  o 521 40556 4 paperback
Pufendorf *On the Duty of Man and Citizen according to Natural Law* (edited by
  James Tully)
  o 521 35980 5 paperback

The Radical Reformation (edited by Michael G. Baylor)
o 521 37948 2 paperback

Rousseau *The Discourses and other early political writings* (edited by
Victor Gourevitch)
o 521 42445 3 paperback

Rousseau *The Social Contract and other later political writings* (edited by
Victor Gourevitch)
o 521 42446 1 paperback

Seneca *Moral and Political Essays* (edited by John Cooper and John Procope)
o 521 34818 8 paperback

Sidney *Court Maxims* (edited by Hans W. Blom, Eco Haitsma Mulier and
Ronald Janse)
o 521 46736 5 paperback

Sorel *Reflections on Violence* (edited by Jeremy Jennings)
o 521 55910 3 paperback

Spencer *The Man versus the State* and *The Proper Sphere of Government*
(edited by John Offer)
o 521 43740 7 paperback

Stirner *The Ego and Its Own* (edited by David Leopold)
o 521 45647 9 paperback

Thoreau *Political Writings* (edited by Nancy Rosenblum)
o 521 47675 5 paperback

Utopias of the British Enlightenment (edited by Gregory Claeys)
o 521 45590 1 paperback

Vitoria *Political Writings* (edited by Anthony Pagden and Jeremy Lawrance)
o 521 36714 X paperback

Voltaire *Political Writings* (edited by David Williams)
o 521 43727 X paperback

Weber *Political Writings* (edited by Peter Lassman and Ronald Speirs)
o 521 39719 7 paperback

William of Ockham *A Short Discourse on Tyrannical Government* (edited by
A. S. McGrade and John Kilcullen)
o 521 35803 5 paperback

William of Ockham *A Letter to the Friars Minor and other writings* (edited by
A. S. McGrade and John Kilcullen)
o 521 35804 3 paperback

Wollstonecraft *A Vindication of the Rights of Men* and *A Vindication of the Rights of
Woman* (edited by Sylvana Tomaselli)
o 521 43633 8 paperback

CPSIA information can be obtained
at www.ICGtesting.com
Printed in the USA
LVHW050611290121
677760LV00011B/248

9 780521 567817